Asian Perspectives on Education for Sustainable Development

This book critically considers what various Asian philosophies can contribute to a more substantive discourse on sustainability education and educational philosophy.

The contributors examine how 'east' and 'west' interact in educational philosophy and practice in Asian contexts. As a collection, they provide a broad view of Asian sustainability thinking that is not dominated by Confucianism, Buddhism, Islam, and post-colonialism, but rather which regards these themes—and other frameworks for sustainable education—as dynamic aspects of Asian contexts, both historically and today. As such, the book invites readers to consider the challenges and opportunities for theorising of sustainability in the philosophy of education, while also critically engaging with the way in which 'Asia' and 'east' are typically understood.

Of interest to those researchers in Asian conceptions of sustainability, this book highlights a series of potential insights in relation to the often-foregrounded perspectives of Global North and western-based frameworks.

The chapters were originally published in *Educational Philosophy and Theory*.

Liz Jackson is an Associate Professor and the Director of the Comparative Education Research Centre at the Faculty of Education at the University of Hong Kong. She is also the President of the Philosophy of Education Society of Australasia. She is the author of *Muslims and Islam in U.S. Education: Reconsidering Multiculturalism* (2014) and *Questioning Allegiance: Resituating Civic Education* (2019). She is currently working on a third book entitled *Against Virtue: The Politics of Educating Emotions*.

Educational Philosophy and Theory

Series Editor: Peter Roberts, University of Canterbury, New Zealand

This series is devoted to cutting-edge scholarship in educational philosophy and theory. Each book in the series focuses on a key theme or thinker and includes essays from a range of contributors. To be published in the series, a book will normally have first appeared as a special issue of *Educational Philosophy and Theory*, one of the premier philosophy of education journals in the world. This provides an assurance for readers of the quality of the work and enhances the visibility of the book in the international philosophy of education community. Books in this series combine creativity with rigour and insight. The series is intended to demonstrate the value of diverse theoretical perspectives in educational discourse, and contributors are invited to draw on literature, art and film as well as traditional philosophical sources in their work. Questions of educational policy and practice will also be addressed. The books published in this series will provide key reference points for subsequent theoretical work by other scholars, and will play a significant role in advancing philosophy of education as a field of study.

Recent titles in the series include:

A Kaleidoscopic View of Chinese Philosophy of Education
Edited by Ruyu Hung

John Dewey's Democracy and Education in an Era of Globalization
Edited by Mordechai Gordon and Andrea R. English

Asian Perspectives on Education for Sustainable Development
Edited by Liz Jackson

Measuring Up in Education
Philosophical explorations for justice and democracy within and beyond cultures of measurement in educational systems
Edited by Steven A. Stolz and R. Scott Webster

Cultivation of Self in East Asian Philosophy of Education
Edited by Ruyu Hung

https://www.routledge.com/Educational-Philosophy-and-Theory/book-series/EPT

Asian Perspectives on Education for Sustainable Development

Edited by
Liz Jackson

Routledge
Taylor & Francis Group
LONDON AND NEW YORK

First published 2020
by Routledge
2 Park Square, Milton Park, Abingdon, Oxon, OX14 4RN

and by Routledge
52 Vanderbilt Avenue, New York, NY 10017

Routledge is an imprint of the Taylor & Francis Group, an informa business

First issued in paperback 2021

British Library Cataloguing-in-Publication Data
A catalogue record for this book is available from the British Library

ISBN13: 978-0-367-35923-2 (hbk)
ISBN13: 978-1-03-208843-3 (pbk)

Typeset in ITC Galliard Std
by codeMantra

Publisher's Note
The publisher accepts responsibility for any inconsistencies that may have arisen during the conversion of this book from journal articles to book chapters, namely the inclusion of journal terminology.

Contents

Citation Information

The chapters in this book were originally published in *Educational Philosophy and Theory*. When citing this material, please use the original page numbering for each article, as follows:

Introduction
'Asian' Perspectives on Education for Sustainable Development
Liz Jackson
Educational Philosophy and Theory, volume 49, issue 5 (May 2017) pp. 473–479

Chapter 1
Ethnic Tourism and the Big Song: Public Pedagogies and the Ambiguity of Environmental Discourse in Southwest China
Jinting Wu
Educational Philosophy and Theory, volume 49, issue 5 (May 2017) pp. 480–500

Chapter 2
Vernadsky meets Yulgok: A non-Western dialog on sustainability
Tamara Savelyeva
Educational Philosophy and Theory, volume 49, issue 5 (May 2017) pp. 501–520

Chapter 3
Rethinking the Concept of Sustainability: Hiroshima as a subject of peace education
Kanako Ide
Educational Philosophy and Theory, volume 49, issue 5 (May 2017) pp. 521–530

Chapter 4
Educating the Heart and the Mind: Conceptualizing inclusive pedagogy for sustainable development
Mousumi Mukherjee
Educational Philosophy and Theory, volume 49, issue 5 (May 2017) pp. 531–549

Chapter 5
No-Self, Natural Sustainability and Education for Sustainable Development
Chia-Ling Wang
Educational Philosophy and Theory, volume 49, issue 5 (May 2017) pp. 550–561

Chapter 6

Harmonizing ecological sustainability and higher education development: Wisdom from Chinese ancient education philosophy
Xiaoxia Chen
Educational Philosophy and Theory, volume 51, issue 11 (October 2019) pp. 1080–1090

For any permission-related enquiries please visit:
http://www.tandfonline.com/page/help/permissions

Contributors

Xiaoxia Chen is a Senior Lecturer of the School of Translation Studies at Qufu Normal University, China. Her research activity has focused on building a perfect learning environment for college students, with particular attention to drawing wisdom from Chinese ancient philosophy.

Kanako Ide is an Associate Professor of the Faculty of Education at Soka University, Tokyo, Japan. Her main research interests are in democratic education, peace education, and patriotic education from a philosophical perspective.

Liz Jackson is an Associate Professor and the Director of the Comparative Education Research Centre at the Faculty of Education at the University of Hong Kong. She is also the President of the Philosophy of Education Society of Australasia.

Mousumi Mukherjee is an Associate Professor and the Deputy Director of the International Institute for Higher Education Research and Capacity Building (IIHEd) at O.P. Jindal Global University, Sonipat, India. She is a Member Secretary of the Research Ethics and Review Board (RERB) and the founding Executive Director of the Centre for Comparative and Global Education (CCGE).

Tamara Savelyeva is an Assistant Professor in the Department of International Education and Lifelong Learning at the Education University of Hong Kong. She teaches philosophy and cultural sociology of education in the Faculty of Education and Human Development.

Chia-Ling Wang is an Associate Professor at the National Taiwan Ocean University. She is both the Chair at the Institute of Education and the Director at the Centre of Teacher Education. Her research interests include philosophy of education, curriculum theories, and higher education.

Jinting Wu is an Assistant Professor of Educational Leadership and Policy at the University at Buffalo, USA. She is a recipient of the 2013 Gail P. Kelly Outstanding Dissertation Award in Comparative Education. Her research interests include comparative education, anthropology of education, educational philosophy, immigrant education, and Chinese diaspora.

INTRODUCTION

'Asian' Perspectives on Education for Sustainable Development

LIZ JACKSON

Consensus among the global elite has recently emerged that key natural resources are finite and that environmental degradation, climate change, and resource scarcity challenge human survival and flourishing and fuel human conflicts (Gadotti, 2008). That humans must change their approach to living on earth or face dire consequences is behind intergovernmental organizations and others' calls for education for sustainable development (ESD). However, as a framework, ESD lacks a substantive foundation in educational research or philosophy. Though philosophers and educators have at times pondered and reflected on the implications of humankind's interrelations with the natural world (e.g. Benson, 2000; Lights & Rolston, 2002), ESD has largely been a political movement, fueled by United Nations and related groups' urgings for action (Hopkins & Mckeown, 2002). As a result, answers to critical questions for implementation remain essentially contested, such as how individuals, societies, and the world should move forward (Blenkinsop, 2013; Gadotti, 2008; Maniates, 2001); how to conceptualize the relationship between humans and the natural world (e.g. Krasny & Roth, 2010; Lundholm & Plummer, 2010); and how educators can change attitudes and/or behaviors related to sustainability (Connolly & Prothero, 2008; Vare & Scott, 2007). Due to the complexity of challenges that are not just environmental but also political and economic, and due to perceived clashes of sustainability and development aims, some argue now that ESD and sustainability are neoliberal buzzwords (Bengtsson & Ostman, 2013; Stevenson, 2007).

In this context, educators and policy-makers have observed that Global North and Western and Western-centered frameworks for exploring ESD have proliferated in comparison with Global South, indigenous, Eastern, and other perspectives. While the challenge of cultivating scholarship and research that is more geographically and culturally inclusive is well known, particularly in philosophy, how diverse perspectives can productively engage fundamental sustainability issues and questions has not been well elaborated. On the other hand, some suspect that it is a part of Western liberalism itself or Christianity that causes sustainability issues to be inadequately conceptualized in Western postindustrial societies. Lynn White posited in 1967 that the Christian view of the earth as a domain for humanity's use has challenged Christian scholars and others coming from Judeo-Christian cultural contexts to cultivate critical environmental understanding. Wapner (1996) and Tamara Savelyeva (in this issue) identify dualisms of mind/body and man/environment as part of the liberal philosophical tradition, wherein Enlightenment was conceived early on partly as ways of productively engaging the material world for the benefit of humanity. It has been a common refrain that Western civilization and Western modes of development have focused on the natural world primarily as resources to the detriment of humanity and animal and plant species for much of modern history, unwittingly disturbing balances beyond human comprehension in order to 'develop' and 'progress'.

Yet, concepts of East/West and North/South should also be problematized as dualisms. And it is necessary to critically examine what Eastern or Southern (as examples) frameworks for sustainability education can contribute, rather than assuming that deep in the jungle lies the answer to ESD's mysteries. In this special issue of *Educational Philosophy and Theory*, scholars explore diverse Asian orientations toward sustainability in education with dialogs of East–West in mind, critically considering what various Asian philosophies could contribute to a more substantive discourse on sustainability education and educational philosophy. These articles do not claim that humanity should go East for direction in this domain, but they examine how East/West can and do interrelate and interact in educational philosophy and practice in specific Asian contexts. As a collection, they provide a broad view of Asian sustainability thinking that is not dominated by Confucianism, Buddhism, Islam, postcolonialism, etc. but regards these themes, and other frameworks for living and education, as dynamic aspects of Asian contexts historically and today. As such, they invite readers to consider challenges and opportunities for future theorizing of sustainability in philosophy of education, while at the same time critically engaging the way 'Asia' is typically understood.

In this short article, I give a brief background to ESD in educational philosophy and practice, before exploring some of the key themes emerging out of the articles in this special issue for theorizing sustainability and sustainability education within and across Asian contexts. I argue, in relation to the articles here, that approaches to West/East and conceptualizations of Asia must be critically engaged when it comes to educational theory, and I frame this topic as one case for developing a better understanding of the dialog of West–East in philosophy of education. Rather than settling the debates mentioned in these pages related to ESD, this issue aims to provide a more critical perspective on the relation of East–West in the 'Asian' world of educational theory. Thus, these pages may be of value to people wondering what Asian sustainability or Asian philosophies of ESD might look like or entail, though they do not formally propose alternative (to Western or global) worldviews or ESD practices rooted in some pure Asian landscape.

ESD, West, and East

In Western ethics and popular awareness, the idea that people should or must take responsibility for conserving the environment and natural resources emerged in the 1970s (Benson, 2000). Naess (1973) and Routley and Routley (1973/1980) voiced a need for ethicists to consider not harming the environment as an important principle akin to not harming humans or their interests directly or indirectly. The International Union for the Conservation of Nature argued at the same time for environmental education to help people to better appreciate the interrelations of human societies and the natural world as a code for behavior (Lee & Efird, 2014). The 1987 Bruntland Report (World Commission on Environment and Development) gave what is today the most widely cited definition of sustainable development, which emphasizes that economic development should not compromise the availability of natural resources needed for future generations. Since the Rio Summit of 1992, ESD has been a major focus of United Nations work to encourage formal and nonformal environmental education across levels of schooling and in community development around the world. The United Nations proclaimed 2005–2015 the 'Decade of Education for Sustainable Development', signaling the importance of ESD across fields and communities worldwide.

In the last few decades, a wide range of terms have been used alongside ESD which emphasize different priorities and approaches, such as eco-pedagogy, education for sustainability, sustainability education, and pedagogy of place. Most approaches ask students to consider how human economic and social and cultural concerns interact with the importance of conservation of natural resources. Therefore, all contemporary approaches to ESD are, at minimum, interdisciplinary, issues based, and topical. But beyond this sort of general and thin conceptualization, best practices and approaches remain contested. Some argue that transmitting knowledge and appropriate values should be the main focus of ESD; others argue that values of peace, social justice, and human flourishing demand a focus on values and skills education that empowers students to engage in dialogs and problem-solving with others, given the scale and dynamism of environmental and sustainability challenges today (Jackson, 2016; Vare & Scott, 2007).

The notion that Western ethics and worldviews are particularly misaligned with environmental ethics and green views that recognize environment and humanity holistically has been articulated regularly in environmental sustainability literature (Benson, 2000; Naess, 1973; Routley & Routley, 1973/1980; Wapner, 1996). As Western ethics has focused on individuals in relation to one another in contrast with Buddhism or Confucianism which foreground holism and communities (respectively), many have posited that these latter views, more influential in many Asian societies, may better facilitate the construction of environmental ethics and effective ESD (Lee & Efird, 2014). Studies comparing environmental attitudes in Western societies to those in Asian societies such as Japan, Korea, Macau, and China have not given strong support to the idea that such cultural values make a difference in people's environmental perceptions and views, however (Jackson et al., 2016; Lee & Efird, 2014). Such simplifications also ignore the potential importance of different economic and political ideologies in contemporary Asian experiences, as well as the educational orientations that remain popular in Asian societies today.

More broadly, such views of Eastern or Asian environmental ethics imply a shallow understanding of 'East' and Asia. As Lewis and Wigen (1997) articulate, Asia should be understood as a concept of human geography rather than physical geography, historically always invoking a dynamic dialectic of East and West of the Eurasian landmass and Asia Pacific region. As Bowring (1987) has noted, the only thing unified by the name of 'Asia', which has always encompassed an incredible diversity of cultures, ethnicities, religions, languages, and lifestyles, is its exclusion from Europe: that is, a negative sense of being non-European. The notion of Asian identity within Asia was reflected historically only within the context of anti-colonial and anti-imperial attitudes; Asians did not see themselves as unified in any other way (Bowring, 1987). And Asian colonial and postcolonial experiences are not particularly similar across the diverse continent and oceanic lands, and are made more complex by the role of colonization by Asian groups themselves. Thus, despite social imaginaries vividly employed within Western contexts (wherein 'Asian American' or 'Asian Australian' refer to particular demographic groups in Western society more often than not), there is no particularly useful way of elaborating 'Asian culture' or an 'Asian view' from within, given the internal diversity and historical East–West dialectics embedded in any so-called Asian contexts.

Dialogs on Sustainability, East and West

The articles in this special issue foreground the status of Asia as an empty signifier, standing in for far more complex relations of East and West, of dialogical, dynamic histories and contemporary realities. They indicate on multiple levels how Asian societies have looked out, to Western ones and one another, just as westerners look East, debunking the notion that any purely Eastern/Asian perspective remains. Tamara Savelyeva's essay, 'Vernadsky meets Yulgok: a Non-Western Dialog on Sustainability', does this most bluntly, juxtaposing historical Eurasian and Asian perspectives on the environment and humanity's role in sustainability, namely the metaphysics of Russian theorist Vladimir Vernadsky, and the Korean neo-Confucianism of Yulgok Yi. Rather than asking readers to employ these historical views in developing contemporary approaches to ESD, Savelyeva illuminates how dialogs of East and West and East and East are no new phenomenon, but are reflected in centuries of comparative and intercultural thought in the Eurasian and Asian world.

An East–West dialectic that rejects a type of purist Asian view is also elaborated in Mousumi Mukherjee's essay, 'Educating the Heart and the Mind: Conceptualizing Inclusive Pedagogy for Sustainable Development'. Reductive views of postcolonialism tend to see colonization as disempowering and oppressive overall, particularly in the Indian context. Yet in Mukherjee's assessment of the work of one school, a historical institution that took on a mission of intercultural integration and increasing equity for disadvantaged Indian youth and girls over time, the value of cross-cultural dialog in envisioning empowering postcolonial institutions is foregrounded. Further, Mukherjee observes how 'theory too must be deimperialized' (quoting Chen, 2010) in understanding diverse Asian educational histories, as the complexity of postcolonial landscapes like India is often made opaque in Western theoretical examinations. A kind of East–West dialog, Mukherjee asserts, is at the heart of the success and impact of one of India's most remarkable educational institutions, from the perspective of sustainability education as education for greater equity and social justice for all.

Similarly, Wu Jinting examines how dialectics of economic development, Western-style commercialization, and local cultural sustainability synchronize, but in this case quite problematically, in the context of an ethnic minority tourism project in contemporary China. As noted previously, some theorists have suggested that sustainability and development are at crossroads rather than being mutually complementary (Bengtsson & Ostman, 2013). In 'Ethnic Tourism and the Big Song: Public Pedagogies and the Ambiguity of Environmental Discourse in Southwest China', Wu provides rich data to elaborate such notions, vividly portraying how a rural ethnic community and its culture has become commercialized as a result of a project aimed at rural indigenous development and sustenance. On the one hand, Chinese tourists are encouraged today to flock to the countryside to appreciate and learn about sustainability, where the air is clean and longstanding cultural traditions remain a part of everyday life. However, to keep tourists coming and open-minded to this form of ESD requires modern sanitation and beautification of the village, and popularization of distinctive historical ethnic folk songs. The community must accept its neighborhood facelift and musical reduction to poppy jingles in order to experience something like its own sustainability. It must change to stay the same or to remain within China oriented paradoxically toward both sustainability and development today.

Kanako Ide bridges contemporary ESD related to caring and peace education of East and West, this case in Japan, in 'Rethinking the Concept of Sustainability: Hiroshima as a Subject of Peace Education'. Focusing on the postwar Hiroshima social, educational, and natural landscape, Ide's essay highlights points of interrelation between Nel Noddings's care and relational theories of education and peace educational philosophy as practiced in understanding environmental degradation and sustainability in contemporary Hiroshima. Though Noddings has not focused on human relations with the natural world in depth in her work, Ide finds significant parallels in view between Noddings's focus on relation with and care for others in education; and the way educators teach against war and for sustainability in Hiroshima today, through helping students understand how they relate to the natural world around them, and can care and be cared for by plant life growing in this site of infamous human and natural tragedy. Like Savelyeva's essay, this article highlights points of similarities across apparently divergent intellectual traditions, emphasizing new opportunities for dialog across East and West.

The final article here (first, as organized in the contents) is 'Self, Natural Sustainability, and Education for Sustainable Development' by Wang Chia-Ling. In this article, Wang reflects on the question raised previously, whether there is something fundamentally more pro-ecological about Asian ways of seeing the world. Evaluating the concept of *no-self* in Buddhism (and *non-action* in Chinese Daoism), Wang argues that there is rich potential in juxtaposing these views with traditional Western ideas of the relationships between environments and individuals. Concluding with remarks for education, Western and Eastern thinkers and philosophers are invoked in her recommendation for mindfulness education. Perhaps the most traditionally styled philosophy of education article in this collection, Wang provides provocations to Western and Buddhist (and Daoist, and other Asian) readers alike here, to consider how their views may correlate or clash in their educational implications and possibilities.

Taken as a whole, these articles reflect that diversity, not uniformity, is part of both Western and Asian philosophies of sustainability and sustainable development; that dialog across and within East and West characterizes so-called 'Asian' theory in this case, rather than any pure Eastern view; and that significant challenges as well as possibilities mark the contemporary theoretical and practical landscape for sustainability and ESD in Asia today. The world can no more rely on a singular and monolithic Asian way or best Eastern practice in the future than it can revert to historical Western conceptions of nature as natural resources and of humanity as in control of the world. As we clearly have all been living together across borders for many centuries despite the notion of 'Asia', not just geographically but also culturally, socially, and politically, it makes little sense to presume separateness, mutual exclusion, and dualism in historical or present-day theorizing. As revealed in these articles, Asian philosophies of ESD are diverse, intersecting with each other and with Western views. Developing a new approach to Asia and East–West relation is vital for productively reflecting upon already existing historical, commonplace dialogs of East and West as discussed here, which can in turn enhance the development of more critical theoretical and practical approaches to ESD that better represent and reflect human vision as a whole.

Acknowledgements

The author wishes to thank the authors for their contributions and patience with the production of this special issue and Michael Peters and Susanne Brighouse for support and expertise with production.

Disclosure statement

No potential conflict of interest was reported by the author.

References

Bengtsson, S. L., & Ostman, L. O. (2013). Globalisation and education for sustainable development: Emancipation from context and meaning. *Environmental Education Research, 19*, 477–498.

Benson, J. (2000). *Environmental ethics*. London: Routledge.

Blenkinsop, S. (2013). The ecological danger of compromise. In C. Mayo (Ed.), *Philosophy of Education Yearbook* (pp. 219–221). Urbana, IL: Philosophy of education society.

Bowring, P. (1987). What is "Asia"? *Far Eastern Economic Review, 135*, 30–31.

Chen, K. (2010). *Asia as method: Toward deimperialization*. Durham, NC: Duke University Press.

Connolly, J., & Prothero, A. (2008). Green consumption: Life-politics, risks and contradictions. *Journal of Consumer Culture, 8*, 117–145.

Gadotti, M. (2008). Education for sustainability: A critical contribution to the Decade of Education for Sustainable Development. *Green Theory & Praxis: The Journal of Ecopedagogy, 4*, 15–64.

Hopkins, C., & Mckeown, R. (2002). Education for sustainable development: An international perspective. In D. Tilbury, R. B. Stevenson, J. Fien, & D. Schreuder (Eds.), *Education and sustainability: Responding to a global challenge* (pp. 13–24). Gland: International Union for Conservation of Nature and Natural Resources.

Jackson, L. (2016). Education for sustainable development: From environmental education to broader views. In E. Railean, G. Walker, A. Elci, & L. Jackson (Eds.), *Handbook of applied learning theory and design in modern education* (pp. 42–65). Hershey, PA: IGI Global.

Jackson, L., Pang, M.-F., Brown, E., Cain, S., Dingle, C., & Bonebrake, T. (2016). Environmental attitudes and behaviors among secondary students in Hong Kong. *International Journal of Comparative Education and Development, 18*, 70–80.

Krasny, M. E., & Roth, W. M. (2010). Environmental education for social-economical system resilience: A perspective from activity theory. *Environmental Education Research, 16*, 545–558.

Lee, J. C.-K., & Efird, R. (Eds.). (2014). *Schooling for sustainable development across the Pacific*. Dordrecht: Springer.

Lewis, M. W., & Wigen, K. (1997). *The myth of continents: A critique of metageography*. Berkeley: University of California Press.

Lights, A., & Rolston, H. (Eds.). (2002). *Environmental ethics: An anthology*. London: Blackwell.

Lundholm, C., & Plummer, R. (2010). Resilience and learning: A conspectus for environmental education. *Environmental Education Research, 16*, 475–491.

Maniates, M. F. (2001). Individualization: Plant a tree, buy a bike, save the world? *Global Environmental Politics, 1*, 31–52.

Naess, A. (1973). The shallow and the deep, long-range ecology movement. A summary*. *Inquiry, 16*, 95–100.

Routley, R., & Routley, V. (1973/1980). Human chauvinism and environmental ethics. In D. Mannison, M. McRobbie, & R. Routley (Eds.), *Environmental philosophy* (pp. 129–131). Canberra: Australian National University.

Stevenson, R. B. (2007). Schooling and environmental/sustainability education: From discourses of policy and practice to discourses of professional learning. *Environmental Education Research, 13*, 265–285.

Vare, P., & Scott, W. (2007). Learning for change: Exploring the relationship between education and sustainable development. *Journal of Education for Sustainable Development, 1*, 191–198.

Wapner, P. (1996). Toward a meaningful ecological politics. *Tikkun, 11*, 21–26.

White, L. (1967). The historical roots of our ecological crisis. *Science, 155*, 1204–1207.

World Commission on Environment and Development. (1987). *Our common future*. New York, NY: Oxford University Press.

Ethnic Tourism and the Big Song: Public Pedagogies and the Ambiguity of Environmental Discourse in Southwest China

Jinting Wu

Abstract

The article examines two forms of public pedagogies in a rural region of Southwest China—tourism and ethnic songs—to illustrate their contested roles in transforming local relations with natural and built environment. While tourism development daily alters the village landscape by spatial intervention, demolition, and construction, the 'landscaping' is both a visual and conceptual device that produces a pleasurable environment as the 'other' and signifies what is tourable and what is to be seen. On the other hand, the echoes of the environment and human-nature relations are central elements in ethnic songs that have been sung for centuries as a major music genre to transmit ancestral, historical, and cultural understandings. Indigenous worldviews and ecological awareness are expressed in songs through imitation of nature and worship of various nonhuman forms of life. The paper argues that a nascent environmentalism and ecological significance of the ethnic songs are increasingly oriented towards instrumental development rationality, while at the same time revived and choreographed in staged tourism performances. Both tourism and ethnic songs offer powerful forms of public pedagogies through which to rethink how incommensurable discourses generate new environmental crises by drastically altering not only the vernacular landscape but also local cosmological beliefs. The short-lived developmental zest and the longstanding local ecological consciousness play out complex dynamics in 'teaching' the locals and the tourists about the changing environment of rural ethnic China, and the ambiguities and tensions that exist within the notion of sustainable development.

Introduction

In 2013, the newly elect Chinese President Xi Jinping highlighted his inaugural speech with an urge for 'ecological civilization' (生态文明). Such urge is to redirect China from a headlong rush to quantitative growth indexed by the volume of GDP to a development model with environmental sustainability. Xi's predecessor Hu Jintao, in the 17th Party Congress in 2007, articulated a similar goal of 'ecological civilization' and a 'green GDP' as a crucial component of the 'scientific development' paradigm (Xinhua Net, 2007). The social costs of environmental degradation as a result of unchecked industrialization have brought China repeated international embarrassment. While growth still remains the priority, the ecological consequences have exploded political debates, injecting a new urgency into China's immediate and long-term future.

For quite some time, China has focused on economic growth to pull hundreds of millions of citizens out of poverty. Ecological systems have been largely conceived as standing reserves for serving human needs. China claimed to be in a developmental stage that necessitated, however unfortunately, certain degree of environmental sacrifice, citing similar lack of attention to the problem of pollution by Western countries during the Industrial Revolution (Pan, 1999, p. 501; Wu, He, Fan, & Zhao, 1998). The practice of 'pollute now and treat later' has been seriously challenged in recent decades. Facing immense environmental crisis, the state has made environmental regulations a top policy matter, investing in wind and solar power, cleaning up contaminated farmlands, incorporating environmental performance in overall evaluation of local officials (Zhang, 2007), and rewarding cities making progress on air pollution.[1] In addition, with worsening pollution, more and more city dwellers engage in environmental-cultural tourism to temporarily move away from urban congestion and set foot on the pristine, rustic, 'out-of-the-way' places (Chio, 2014; Oakes, 2006). Tourism travels accentuate the urban–rural divide and produce ambiguous environmental discourses in rural China, a focal point of discussion in this paper.

Environmental tourism presents a different gesture for thinking about human–nature interdependence, promoted by the Chinese state as a strategy of sustainable development (Zhuang, Lassoie, & Wolf, 2011). It also enacts a particular logic of difference by presenting the rural as the modern-day escape with clear waters, fresh air, and verdant mountains in contrast to the steel-and-concrete, carbon-dioxide-filled urban sphere. The environmental ethics in certain rural ethnic communities, such as the Kam people in this study, is increasingly touted in tourism programs as welcomed alternatives of sustainable living. With the promotion of tourism and the rising visibility of the Kam singing, the Kam villagers in Southwest China became known for their environmental stewardship in protecting the ecosystem as the spiritual habitat of both humans and other forms of beings.

This paper examines tourism and ethnic songs as two forms of public pedagogies in a minority Kam community in Southwest China to illustrate their contested roles in transforming local relations with natural and built environment. The term 'pedagogy' used in this article, inspired by the works of Paulo Freire (1995) and critical scholars such as Henry Giroux (1988), regards education as a broad genre of practices involving wider domains of social existence and cultural politics, rather than merely confined in formal schooling. Tourism and ethnic songs, I argue, play a central educative role in 'teaching' the locals and the tourists about the changing environment of rural ethnic China, and the ambiguities and tensions that exist within the notion of sustainable development. In addition, the paper proposes a place-based pedagogy to nurture bonds with local contexts, foster critical understanding of the environmental aspects of social development, and build ecological thinking in China's educational landscape.

The Kam community in this study is located in Guizhou, one of the least-developed provinces populated mainly by ethnic minorities and described in a popular proverb as 'a place without three acres of flat lands, three days of fine weather, or three cents to rub together.' The language of poverty and remoteness prevails in public and policy reports to construct this region on the lower end of the development pole. Environmental discourses in rural ethnic communities of Guizhou Province are thus tied to the imperative of economic development, a growing tourism industry, and indigenous[2] cosmologies and ecological views used as the marketing ploy of ecotourism. My paper examines how the neoliberal development agenda produces contested environmental discourses and values, shaping the ethnic rural environment both physically and symbolically. Furthermore, the paper argues for place-based pedagogies to bear on the well-being of the environment people inhabit and to challenge the absence of an ecological dimension in educational discourse.

State-led development programs tout tourism as a pillar of rural poverty reduction. While tourism development seeks to aestheticize the village landscape by spatial alteration and demolition, the 'landscaping' is both a conceptual and physical device to transform the material conditions of rural life and produces a pleasurable environment as the 'other.' Tourism enables a neoliberal framing of the countryside, calling on both the landscape and its residents to 'perform' in accordance to the market logic. The farmers are called upon to become self-entrepreneurial and pull themselves up through their own bootstraps, so to speak. As well, the appearance of the rural environment becomes a site of governing that needs to be groomed to boost urban leisure and increase rural income. Rural environment is marketed as harmonious coexistence of nature and humans, as welcomed alternative to urban living. However, the newfangled village-scape conceals tourism's intrusion on local lives and the backstage spatial contestations, and turns a blind eye to the rich ecological understanding distilled in folk songs, a point to which I will return shortly.

Meanwhile, the echoes of the environment and human–nature relations are central to Kam ethnic songs that have been sung for centuries to transmit ancestral, historical, and cultural understandings. Ethnic singing indicates a unique identity of the Kam, marketed in the branding of ecotourism in Qiandongnan. Within Southeast Guizhou, different genres of traditional Kam songs are sung on different occasions, such as wedding, funeral, and New Year, to celebrate indigenous histories and customs. More importantly, the Kam songs express an ecological consciousness and a celebration of nature through the lyrical contents of mountains, birds, plants, seasons, farming, and various nonhuman forms of life. As I will discuss, a nascent environmentalism captured in ethnic songs are increasingly diluted by the instrumental use of singing as 'tourist entertainment' while at the same time selectively revived in choreographed stage performances. Both tourism and ethnic songs offer powerful forms of public pedagogies to rethink how incommensurable discourses generate new environmental dilemmas by altering the vernacular landscape and trivializing local ecological system. While curricula in rural schools are chiefly urban oriented, a place-based critical pedagogy, if properly invoked, might provide some transformative educational responses to increase the awareness of the indigenous knowledge system and address the neoliberal impacts on rural ecological well-being.

The Place, the People, and the Ethnographic Context

The research is situated in mountainous Guizhou, China's border region fitting James Scott's description of a 'shatter zone' (2009) populated by diverse ethnic groups at the margins of state control. For past centuries, Guizhou's ethnic residents have been perceived as barbarian, uncivilized, or at best, culturally distinct from the Han Chinese (Oakes, 1998). The structural marginalization of ethnic minorities has been criticized as China's 'internal Orientalism' (Schein, 2000) that sorts different ethnicities on a developmental hierarchy. The Kam people in Guizhou are generally considered pacifist, quaint, and nonconfrontational, rather than antagonistic to the Chinese state as other ethnic groups (such as the Tibetan and Uyghur people) are sometimes perceived. In recent decades, tourism-centered development model is gaining popularity in Guizhou, especially with its rich natural resources, distinct ethnic lifeways and cultural heritage (see Chio, 2014). In Qiandongnan Prefecture (Southeast Guizhou) in particular, new roads have led to considerable growth of domestic tourism since the 1990s (Oakes, 1998, p. 169). Rural tourism becomes an essential part of the state initiative to 'build a new socialist countryside,' bolstered by the naming of 'Ecotourism Year' (1999) and 'Year of Rural Tourism' (2006). Today, discourses of incivility are largely replaced by narratives of empowerment, which aim to uplift rural minorities from poverty. However, a historicist style of reasoning is still palpable in state programs that discursively construct the rural environment as the ideal periphery or 'decorative edge' to the modern Chinese nation, and accentuate the otherness of ethnic cultural heritage, such as singing, as tourist attraction. Exploring the ambiguity of environmental discourse in Southwest China reveals particular paradoxes and power relations in contemporary China. Investigating power relations in the rural situated context can illuminate the linkage of ecological themes with critical themes (such as social inequality, neoliberalism, and global capitalism) to bring about a critical pedagogy of place with the goal of social transformation.

The Kam people (or Dong 侗 in Chinese) in this study occupy the lower plains along the Duliu River in the Qiandongnan Miao and Dong Autonomous[3] Prefecture (黔东南苗族侗族自治州) in Guizhou, and are known for their love and virtuosity of polyphonic singing. Historically, the Kam people have depended upon subsistence agriculture of wet-rice cultivation, which is supplemented by husbandry, artisanal occupations (such as carpentry and stone masonry), and in recent decades, factory work and tourism. Presently, the Kam has a population of 3 million, found primarily in Guizhou (55%), Hunan (28%), and Guangxi (10%) provinces (Cornet, 2009,

p. 195). My field site Longxing[4] is a village-town tucked away in the locally revered Mt. Sasui at the bottom of an enclosed valley. With 4000 or so inhabitants living in some 800 households, it is promoted as a tourist destination for its idyllic scenery, distinct Kam lifeways, and resounding melodies of the polyphonal singing. In tourism brochures, the vernacular landscape is often combined with ethnic cultural elements, featuring fully attired Kam people (usually young females) tilling the fields and singing joyfully on mountain terraces. Such photographic representation constructs a particular environmental discourse with a smooth synthesis of culture and nature, as if suggesting certain ethnic groups are inextricably linked to the environment as the symbol of harmony.

In seeking to attract domestic tourists, an external company called *Fenghua* wielded exclusive power to develop a theme-park style of ethnic culture *mis en spectacle* in Longxing, often to the locals' discontent. What is known as the 'Chinese Style Tourism' (Stanley, 1998) weaves together a mixture of landscape, architecture, and performance to create particular experience for the visitors. As Nyíri (2006, p. 68) remarks, for Chinese tourists, 'landscape is experienced not so much for 'its own' sake as it is a sign for a set of cultural references,' while 'performance, not 'everyday life' is expected and appreciated.' Indeed, 'the Chinese Style Tourism' typifies Longxing through exhibited landscape, architecture, displays, and performances, 'teaching' the visitors what is to see and 'instructing' the locals to brand their 'otherness' and 'difference' as commodity. As Freire (1995) argues, being in a situation has a spatial, contextual, and pedagogical dimension. Tourism is such a situation where both visitors and locals learn to experience or act upon a place in particular ways.

For many urban travelers who set foot in Longxing for the first time, the village may well appear exotic, with the drum towers, the wind-and-rain bridges (also called roofed-bridges or flower-bridges), the opera stages, the Ganlan-style houses stacked zigzag like mossy pancakes, and a scenic river meandering through the village (see Figure 1). Due to the recent tourism boom, Longxing has become the socioeconomic magnet for the surrounding region, attracting people from near and far to come and work as shopkeepers, vegetable vendors, and hotel staff. Migrants have also returned from the cities, lured by the hope of making it through 'doing tourism' (搞旅游) at home. Indeed, marketization has become a modus operandi in shaping village livelihood. By the beginning of 2000s, Longxing had been featured in national and regional newspapers, guidebooks, and tourism websites, named as 'one of the six most charming ancient towns in China' by the Chinese National Geographic Magazine and 'the top 33 most appealing tourist destinations in China' by the American Fashion magazine and the National Geographic Magazine. In addition, the ecological village museum (生态博物馆) jointly established by Norway and China in the neighboring village Tang'an (see Figure 2) brought more tourists to Longxing. In 2010, the Kam Grand Choir (侗族大歌) was enlisted as the UNESCO Intangible Cultural Heritage, which gave a further boost to the Kam music-making and brought greater visibility to the region and the ethnic group.

I spent 16 months in Qiandongnan between 2009 and 2010, when tourism development was at its peak, to study educational dilemmas facing rural minority

Figure 1: Distant view of village Longxing's residential cluster

Figure 2: Sister village Tang'an nestled amidst lush rice terraces

communities in Southwest China. During the sojourn, I participated in many aspects of the village life, learning to speak the local variant of the Kam language, recording songs with tribal elders, volunteer-teaching at the village schools, taking part in social festivities. My research is ethnographic in nature, drawing upon participant observation, interviews, and informal discussions with a range of personas in different age, gender, and status groups (including teachers, bureaucrats, tourists, students, parents, and song experts). Doing ethnography afforded me lengthy immersion in the village to gain a situated understanding of the rich ecological ethics of the Kam people and the shifting meanings of the environment at the crossroads of rural development.[5] The concept of environment as used here refers to the geographic surrounding of a particular locale, the lived habitat of a people, as well as the spiritual/cosmological space in which humans, animals, and plants function. Critical scholarship of popular culture shows that consumption of various kinds (such as soap operas, TV, magazines, retail malls) can be a critical site of informal learning (Armstrong, 2005; Tisdell & Thompson, 2006). Rural environment is also a site of consumption, of conflicts, of negotiations where folk ecologies are juxtaposed with market logic to provide ongoing learning and meaning-making. Understanding the multiple, contesting environmental discourses in the Kam community is integral to understanding the changing physical, material, and social conditions of ethnic Guizhou, which can enable a community-engaged pedagogy to examine the inherent power relations and complex effects of tourism development on local environment.

Landscaping and Place-making: Tourism as the Ballads of Rural Development

Tourism plays an important role in the place-making of Qiandongnan, noted as key to 'solving the problems relating to agriculture, the countryside, and the farmers' (Cornet, 2009, p. 197). Posed as 'problems,' the countryside is socially constructed through discourses of distance that keep 'the rural' at once central to the overall development and peripheral at the edge of the nation. Tourism-related environmental discourse corresponds to such center–periphery paradox at work to both maintain the distance of the rural as attractive destination and promote its connectedness through domestic travel. A new rural-ethnic-scape is marketed as harmonious coexistence of nature and humans to satisfy city dwellers' desire for a brief respite from hectic, polluted urban spaces. Tourism enables the aestheticization of the rural, donning the vernacular landscape with price tags and reconfiguring the rural spaces with neoliberal consumer logics.

The physicality of rural environment comes to serve as a crucial template in the production of tourist imagination. In Longxing, local governments invested heavily in altering its physical appearance through a 'face-lift' by signing a 50-year contract with an external corporate *Fenghua* and granting it exclusive control on tourism development. The demolition and construction peaked in early 2009 as Longxing was getting ready for the propaganda event of One Conference Two Festivals (一会两节),[6] for which it was chosen as the main site. According to the master plan jointly designed by the local government and the developer, pebbled roads would be paved throughout the village, scenic spots would be designated and signs put up, hotels would be established, a performance square and business road would be built, ticket houses would be installed at gates to sell park entries, and peasants would convert their houses into Farmers' Happiness (农家乐, i.e. family-restaurant-cum-inns) for tourists to experience 'the authentic' rural life. Meanwhile, the construction of an interprovincial highway and a railway nearby was in full force, sending many project managers and construction workers to tour, dine, and shop at the village market. Local Kam villagers also saw tourism as an opportunity to improve their livelihood, yet the initial enthusiasm waned as daily lives were intervened, as tourism proceeds didn't seem to trickle down, and as the ancestral heritage and environment was subject to greater changes and uncertainties.

With visual façade considered vital for tourism success, new houses were required to be painted in dark hues and bricks covered with tree barks to create a sense of antiquity. Additionally, to the locals' dismay, houses violating the scenic spot architectural standards would be torn down; housedogs and wondering chicken were prohibited for 'sanitation' and 'aesthetics' concerns; communal Drum Towers and Wind-and-Rain-Bridges were wired with neon bulbs and dressed up like artificial Christmas trinkets. Villagers were upset to see their living environment meddled with by corporate hands, which to them would create bad karma and invite misfortune. While commercial developers and officials frowned upon such beliefs as superstition, they turned a blind eye to the ways vernacular environment was conceived by the Kam as the fountainhead of livelihood populated and guarded by ancestral spirits and deities. The rhetoric of local sacrifice for regional progress[7] reinforces a neoliberal environmental discourse that has not only drastically altered village landscape, but also undermined the ways Kam villagers relate to their lands and natural environment, leaving the locals understandably anguished.

Corporate merchants joining hands with government bureaucrats now defined the public space as one in which private profits trumped social needs. Critical scholars (see Giroux, 2004; Sandlin & Milam, 2008) have written about the ways in which neoliberal consumerism, wedded to a belief that market should be the organizing principle of social life, serves a public pedagogy to shape cultural production and redefine common goods into private profit-seeking. The sites of public pedagogy are not restricted to classrooms and school settings, but operate within a wide range of social institutions, such as digital media, entertainments, local cultural heritage, mass tourism, and the like, to produce narratives, images, and modes of existence not always in congruity. The public pedagogy of tourism has given rise to environmental concerns, but also opportunities for the local community to make sense of the impact of economic development on indigenous knowledge and ecological system. As tourism accentuated material desires and promises, many villagers desired for a share of the profit, yet were also deeply conflicted by the turning of their social world into one of spectatorship. They complained of the destructive aspects of commercial encroachment on rural environmental well-being, in that village life was no longer like village life:

> If you were here twenty years ago, you would see firewood neatly stacked up in front of each house. Villagers were proud of the exhibition of their hard work. Now we are forbidden to put anything in front of our house; pretty soon cows and horses will not be allowed to pass through the main street.

Place-making is inherently political. Rather than tapping into the extant funds of local knowledge, village tourism left farmlands requisitioned, mountain terrains drilled through, and everyday rural life sanitized and repackaged to generate pleasure and profits. This echoes the process by which theme parks of various types (such as the Disneyland) rapidly proliferate in many parts of the word, where the presentation of spectacles/symbols becomes a key element in tourism and other consumption activities (Bryman, 2004; Dorfman & Mattelart, 1975). The growing influence of themed environment in settings such as restaurants, hotels, shops, and tourist destinations indicates the increasing prominence of 'branding and theming' in public culture today, which not only shapes human activities, but also the physical, social, and cultural attributes of a place. The village beautification in Longxing is part of the 'theming' that provides a spectacle of the rural environment to 'instruct' the tourists what is to be seen and the locals what is marketable.

The public pedagogy of tourism produces the village landscape as sanitized emblems of the past to cater for urban nostalgia and holiday-making. However, perhaps unaware to the tourists, the vernacular landscape is also a working landscape that involves strenuous subsistence labor, and a spiritual artery that connects the living with the ancestors, the present and the past. The landscape is key to the maintenance of social relations across the generational, spiritual, and species boundaries. Farmlands and mountains are significant—and even 'sacred'—commodities in the Kam village society. The Kam people spoke with awe of the legends about Mt. Sasui and admired in epic songs its undulating hills, layered rice paddies, and densely packed virgin forests. They named newborns after the environment, such as fields, plants, fruits, to remind themselves of Nature's bounty and the otherwise unpredictable agrarian livelihood. However, the pedagogy of tourism remains at the level of spectacles, leaving unchallenged the performative labor and power struggles and diluting the richly intimate rural milieu with commercial rationality.

In the Kam polytheistic belief, all things—living or inanimate—possess certain spiritual essence regardless of their physical forms; spirit pervades all realms of life; all beings are connected; when one allows damage to occur to other beings on earth, one is ultimately incurring damage to oneself. Ancestral worship is a common ritual practiced by the Kam who believe one's ancestors continue to take interests in this-worldly affairs and exert influences on the fortune of the living. In addition, emblems of animals such as fish and birds are woven into the Kam architectures and costumes as the totems of life and prosperity; bridges are worshipped as symbolic pathways connecting life and death. Certain trees (such as Ginkgo biloba) are revered as divine protectors of the communities, as villagers tie straw knots to pay homage to the arboreal gods and prevent them from sabotage (Min & Zhang, 2008; Yang, 2014).

In other words, the sacred commodities of mountains, bridges, and the larger environmental surroundings invoke a different sense of exchangeability. They are signs par excellence of what may be called 'an economy of relations,' of the awareness of human limitations in the greater scheme of things, and of the essential bonds that hold the community together. The exchange value lies in the potency held for retribution and benediction where the debts incurred in this earthly life could be redeemed through extraterrestrial interventions. Material life could not function without acknowledging its indebtedness to the cosmic sphere of beings, and profits could not only be calculated in monetary terms.

This ecological awareness offers a pedagogy of place through which the Kam people can make sense of the environment and devise a locally situated development plan, yet tourism, on the other hand, propagates market-sanctioned ecological values and enables the landscape to 'perform' in line with the logic of profit-making. The neoliberal production of the themed environment is anything but innocent, functioning pedagogically to redefine the ideal rural-scape as comfortably nostalgic, quaint, and peaceful, obscuring the heavy-handed corporate manipulation and the local struggles with mechanisms of control and surveillance. Whether it is the drilling of mountains for highway construction, converting farmlands into tourist venues, or altering vernacular spaces to promote aesthetics of 'authenticity,' the spatial regime of tourism has left the livelihood of many Kam rural households uninsured. Despite the diminishing importance of agriculture and the increasing visibility of waged income, land still constitutes a spatial and spiritual nexus connecting to ancestral heritages and indigenous genealogies, linking the old and the new. Land-based agricultural activities and the rural mountainous landscape feature widely in Kam lyrics, as suggested by the following song:

> … The first month comes around, springtime returns
> The almanac tells us to prepare the field to plant
> Plants and *nyang lak* [singing birds and insects] tell us to dig the field
> From our gains, in the future we will have rice-stores full of rice[8]

Lands are often accorded deep social, moral, and emotional values. To this day, the Kam people in Qiandongnan continue to attach great importance to farming and believe that those who know how to live off of the land can survive better in the rainy days. In Longxing, villagers were called upon to cooperate with the spatial regime of tourism where more rice fields came under commercial commands. Two aspects of farmlands become increasingly contested in environmental discourses in Longxing: firstly, terraced rice fields are an important feature of Kam vernacular landscape that are promoted as a tourist attraction and visual representation of the 'rural look.' The aesthetic potential of the terraces continues to drive tourism in greater Longxing area today, seen in the picturesque cascades of terraces in sister village Tang'an (Figure 2). Secondly, in order to build highways and tourism venues (such as performance square and shopping streets), the local government requisitioned more rice fields, granting negligible amounts of compensation[9] (much lower than the market price) to peasants whose lands were taken. In distress, Kam farmers lamented what to pass on to the next generation now that many of them were landless and tourism profits didn't seem to trickle down.[10] Tourism has undermined the moral significance and sustaining capacities of farmlands, redefining local environmental consciousness with a neoliberal narrative of development.[11] The pedagogy of tourism physically and conceptually subjugates local lands and resources to commercial domination, yoking Kam farmers' relationship with the total environment (human and nonhuman) to the cash nexus of market production.

Meanwhile, road construction has become a prime development strategy of the state to alleviate remoteness of many satellite villages in Guizhou. Paved roads and highways would bring goods, technologies, and ease of travels, yet villagers were also apprehensive of their sabotage of the spiritual arteries of the mountain, infringing upon the mountain gods and inviting bad karma to the living, especially when the local knowledge was not consulted. Tourism did not, and would not, regulate the villagers' own sense of profits and the value they placed on the spiritual, environmental domain. From my observation, the village people resisted seizure of mountain lands not only because they mistrusted the ways the developers manipulated their collective resources, but also because of their belief in the numerous deities that populated the landscape as the wellspring of life energy and whose *guanxi* must be properly maintained. What 'local knowledge' entails is always a historical production and social articulation of place and identity; and in the Kam village, it is the distinct environmental awareness as practiced in everyday livelihood strategies and folk arts (such as singing). However, the local is not a static concept tied to a provincial set of beliefs and practices; nor is caring for the environment only a local matter, significant only to the Kam villagers themselves. The expense of short-term economic gains would eventually be borne by the larger social domains beyond the immediate village community and multiply registered at the local–national–global scale.

The heavy-handed spatial alteration was felt acutely and became a common form of social distress. Even the primary school and the middle school in Longxing were forced to relocate, as the corporate developer intended to seize their prime locations for business ventures. The elderly members in the Kam village were worried about tourism's omnipresent dealings of their living spaces. Even the young followed the exchanges of the adults enthusiastically, whispering that the chosen sites of the new schools were haunted. The apprehension was interpreted, on the part of the commercial developers and state bureaucrats, as foolhardy obstruction of the region's economic future, reinforcing the stereotype that rural folks lacked development visions and were held back by their own outdated world views. Neoliberal development agendas conceive humans primarily as rational, self-interested, future-directed actors, who make decisions in the sole interests of economic profit. The public pedagogy of tourism 'instructs' the Kam villagers to become the neoliberal *homo economicus* and at the same time reinforces their 'backwardness' through belittling local resistance as irrational, superstitious and obstructionist. Attempts to explain such resistance away as forms of backwardness are a condescending reproduction of a particular politics of value that deepens binaries, turns a blind eye to the regenerative potential of rich cosmological worlds of gods and mysticism, and ruthlessly discredits the environmental consciousness already nascent in the ethnic lifeways.

Resonance of the Environment in the Big Songs

The significance of the environment to the Kam people is not only manifested in the conflicts with tourism agendas, but also captured in songs and echoed through the popular, everyday act of singing. Aspects of the natural environment and ecological features are used both literally and metaphorically in songs to express the sentiments, world views, and practical knowledge of the Kam people. The references to the sounds and images of plants, animals, and the natural environment are widely found in 'river songs (in Kam, *ga nya*),' 'going to the mountains songs (*ga bai jin*),' 'drinking songs (*ga kwao*),' and even courting songs sung to initiate romantic relations. The big song, in particular, provides additional ways in which the environment is emphasized and echoed. Known as *Kgal Laox* in Kam and *dongzu dage* (侗族大歌) in Chinese, the 'big songs' (known in English) are usually sung by a group of same-sex singers, composed of two vocal parts (one lower and one higher), unaccompanied, and never conducted. The big song genre has been recognized as a form of National Intangible Cultural Heritage in 2006 and included on UNESCO'S List of the Intangible Cultural Heritage of Humanity in 2009 for its cultural significance as well as uncertainty of future transmission.

With the rise of ethnic tourism and the heritage industry, big songs become a symbol of the pan-Kam identity performed in different staged contexts both domestically and internationally, and featured in televised broadcasts and commercial VCDs or DVDs. Recordings of traditional music on audiocassettes, CDs, and DVDs were made by a range of local, nonlocal, and semiprofessional Kam artists, and targeted for both intra-ethnic and tourism consumption. Kam singing performed to the tourists and distributed through digital media today is increasingly tailored to the modern aesthetic taste and often involve artistic supervision from urban choreographers. In addition, elderly song experts were replaced by youthful, pop-style singers trained with limited song repertoires in order to attract tourists. The forms of music representation tourists encounter are selectively packaged, diluting and trivializing ethnic ecological understanding in consumable forms. But let me first examine the important social and environmental values of ethnic singing to foreground the discussion.

The song-loving Kam people used to proudly state that their children learn to sing before they can talk. As the Kam language is without written scripts, songs are repositories of ethnic histories, agricultural information, tribal laws, and practical advice, sung in a tonal language[12] quite distinct from Mandarin Chinese. It is customary for the Kam to celebrate the Lunar New Year and other festive occasions, such as harvest, by holding singing contests in the village *dare low* (or drum tower 鼓楼 in Chinese), a multi-eaved, pagoda-shaped wooden tower where public gathering, sacrificial rituals, and entertainment take place. In my oral history interviews, the following image was repeatedly described by Kam elders: in the past, after a day of strenuous labor, the Kam, old and young alike, would gather around in the village *dare low* to enjoy a song exchange between a female singing group and a male singing group, or among singing groups of different tribes as they sat opposite each other around an intimate charcoal fire. They sang songs mimicking water gurgling, cicadas chirping, and rooster crowing to soothe fatigue as well as to express their tender feelings.

Songs also served an important function in courtship among unmarried youth who communicated their admiration of one another through intricate lyrics and melodies. The Dong proverb 'Foods nurture the body; songs nurture the heart' (饭养身歌养心) well depicts the existential values of singing. In the Kam language, singing is literally 'doing songs' (*dor kgal*), an intricate part of daily activities that people naturally 'do.' The big song is a living art form and also a pedagogical tool in the Kam society that transmit across generations ethnic folklores, customs, social responsibilities, and other local knowledge including that concerning the environment. In the 1986 debut at the Golden Autumn Arts Festival in France, the Kam big song singing gained prominence as the 'crystal creeks of oriental symphony,' and has since appeared in various national and international media. Since 2000, the big song genre has received increased publicity in tourism promotion as a symbol of the pan-Dong identity (Ingram, 2011).

According to ethnomusicologist Ingram (2011, pp. 445–451), three types of environmental contents perform certain pedagogical functions in the big song genre: the instructional features of environmental management; the use of ecological elements as lyrical metaphors; the vocal imitation of sounds from the natural environment. While the instructional songs illustrate environmental management as practical farming techniques (such as water irrigation and the use of algae to feed domestic pigs), lyrical metaphors involving the natural environments represent the Kam people's philosophical musings (such as the use of plant life as the metaphor for human life, the invoking of timelessness of mountains, water, trees to signify the transient feature of human existence). On the other hand, the imitation of the sounds of water, birds, and insects is used to describe the intimate surroundings and provoke particular sentiments. The echo of the environment in the big song is also an echo of the Kam cosmological belief that holds a sense of 'oneness' between the human and the natural world. The oneness is celebrated through the mimicking of sonic, visual, or experiential environment, through learning and drawing wisdom from the environment, and through the intimate symbiosis depicted in songs between humans and the physical environment, its plant and animal species. As a song goes:

> … Heavy rain and waters rush out of the hole in the field
> Lots of baby fish are lifted out of the water
> After this life we are lifted on to the next
> I am like a *ba beng* [fish] that cannot bear to leave the *weng* [fish]
> We see our friends go to *bak shoy-ee* [in-between world]
> And don't know which place they are taken to [for the next life]
> When friends die first, we feel unsettled and troubled
> [Knowing] later it will be our turn
> And perhaps we will find ourselves in a filthy, manure-filled cow pen
> We have food to eat and clothes to wear
> So we shouldn't be stingy
> We see the Emperor in Imperial Court
> Later he too will provide fertilizer for the grass
> The life of a person is not long
> If you don't sing, it is a real pity[13]

The Kam cosmo is one of reciprocity in which animals, humans, and spirits coexist and are mutually communicable and transformative in ateleological ways. Big song singing provides a sonic representation of the indigenous ecological consciousness and the embodied/emotive ties with the environmental sphere. Singing connects place with self and community, reflecting an indigenous educational philosophy that emphasizes place as a primary experiential context and that is broader than learning of disciplinary content and technological skills as in dominant educational practices.

Indigenous understanding and intimate familiarity with the environment become increasingly contested in recent decades. While tourism and the heritage industry have accentuated the significance of singing, such processes have altered the content and style of Kam songs markedly. Firstly, adapting village singing for staged performance usually involves professional composers, singers and artistic directors from outside and the selective altering of the indigenous musical aspects (such as lyrics and melody) to the aesthetic preferences of a broader audience (usually non-Kam). Secondly, the repertoire of Kam songs has also changed, as shorter, more melodically appealing songs were favored and new songs with relatively superficial lyrics (rather than with dense lyrical complexity) were introduced through staged performances or tourist encounters (Ingram, 2012). During my fieldwork in Longxing, villagers and school children were often recruited and trained ad hoc to perform ethnic songs and lifeways in tourism events (see Figure 3). In the past, villagers formed singing groups to learn a repertoire of songs from a song expert (*geshi* in Chinese or *sang ga* in Kam). Throughout the year, they paid in-kind donations to the *sang ga*, such as gifts and shared meals, and the learning took place in the house of the *sang ga* in the evenings

Figure 3: Public performance staged by students and village performers

after daily farm labor. In recent decades, with labor out-migration, compulsory schooling, and influence of popular culture and mass media, Kam villagers are no longer actively participating in learning songs to any great extent, though singing is still an important part of Kam cultural identities. A song expert in Longxing lamented:

> Twenty years ago, you could hear sounds of singing every night. Singing was the only form of entertainment for us. Everybody could sing, including children. Now you hear tourists singing karaoke or villagers singing drinking songs for them.

Today, tourism performance becomes a predominant way through which village young people come to experience and acquire their folk arts. While an expanding tourism market has stimulated Kam village officials and intellectuals to devote more efforts to preserving and revitalizing ethnic singing, such efforts redirect the traditional art forms towards consumer tastes, and trivialize the environmental values of songs. Folk singing in Longxing is reduced to a set of standard rituals performed by the development company *Fenghua*'s team. For instance, welcoming ceremonies compose of a road-blocking song, where guests are 'blocked' at the village gate and invited to drink the locally brewed rice wine before they are granted entry to the village. Afterwards, tourists proceed to the Drum Tower where more performance and singing are staged with elaborately attired young women and men, trained by the company to deliver a limited repertoire of songs and dances. At local restaurants, drinking songs will also be sung to showcase Kam hospitality and encourage the guests to enjoy local delicacies and rice wine. To the distress of local song teachers, the Company's team altered the lyrics and melodies of the songs to make them more elaborate, whereas villagers' own performance was outcompeted for being true to Kam ethnic singing, rather than accommodating to market tastes (Cornet, 2012, p. 189). While big song singing relates directly to local experience of the environment, singing appropriated in tourism performs a different pedagogical function to teach the tourists what is worth listening and the villagers what should be sung. Furthermore, the sanitized and prescribed tourist experiences symbolically redefine rural environment as one of leisure and consumption, negligent of rich domains of folk ecologies distilled in variegated songs, as well as the contestations and struggles behind the production of tourism façade.

While Longxing has been turned into a theme-park village, the rise of tourism has turned Kam songs, to some extent, into commercial activities (such as restaurant singing) and staged performance (by villagers or professional troupes) as part of a cultural display and public spectacle (Luo, 2010, p. 126). The role of the state in supporting the local traditions of singing has been miniscule, except for the nomination of some Kam singers as *dongge chuanchengren* (transmitters of Kam songs), and in the rhetoric support of incorporating ethnic cultural elements (such as song singing) into school curricula. The indigenous ecological understanding, a deeply meaningful aspect of culture heritage and eco-tourism, remains marginalized and largely overshadowed by the neoliberal pedagogy of the market.

It's worth noting how market influence is interwoven with formal schooling in the transmission of ethnic customs. Public schooling in Qiandongnan is largely centered on Han cultural values, with Mandarin Chinese as the primary language used for instruction,[14] textbooks, and exams. Although minority language and culture is officially recognized in Compulsory Education Law of the PRC (1986, Article 6), state administrative and funding supports in teacher training or curricular development are often inadequate or nonexistent. In Longxing, the rise of ethnic tourism has spurred the county government to implement an initiative for incorporating ethnic culture and history into the classrooms (民族文化进课堂). Yet, transfers of funds to village schools was often delayed or dried up in the lengthy bureaucratic pipelines. In reality, ethnic cultural class was either not taught or taught in a perfunctory manner because it is not a subject of exam and often underfunded. At best, ethnic class was seen as extracurricular activities that added to the teachers' workloads. While the Ministry-authorized national curriculum has little room for non-testing subjects, Kam village children came into contact with ethnic culture and folk learning (such as singing) primarily through tourism. Not infrequently, school children in Longxing were enlisted to stage a singing show to entertain audit-conducting educational officials or tourist delegations. In a way, the public pedagogy of tourism plays a more powerful role than the official pedagogy of formal schooling in socializing village youth with ethnic customs, such as singing, yet in a truncated manner and commercialized setting.

Conclusion

Since the early 1980s, China's market reforms have entailed, and to some extent enabled, the increasing commercial exploitation of natural resources. The neoliberal mandate of growth has intertwined with an urgent sense of environmental crisis in contemporary China. Environmental-cultural tourism has been lauded as a formula to both satisfy urban desire for environmental alternatives and boost rural economic progress. Vernacular rural environment thus occupies a liminal space: on the one hand, it signifies urban travelers' nostalgic longing for the rustic bygones and cleaner environment; on the other hand, it serves a powerful metaphor for the rural–urban developmental chasm and provokes a sense of constraint that prevents ethnic villagers from acquiring market success and experiencing the 'outside world.' As well, rural environment is indispensable to narrative songs and integral to ethnic cultural heritage and the nascent ecological consciousness. Environmental discourses in Qiandongnan are multifaceted; the study of their contested meanings can yield public dialogs and critical understanding of the changing rural–urban relations and the complex ecological, cosmological, and social dynamics in rural Kam society.

This article proposes a broad consideration of 'pedagogy' and 'literacy' with relation to place. Progressive educators attach a great deal of importance to place (Freire, 1995; Dewey, 1938) and consider it as a discursive social construction intertwined with power relations, rather than a neutral geographic entity. Ethnic tourism and big song singing are performative elements of the place, part of the cultural production in the Kam village. As this article shows, both tourism and songs are place-based pedagogical tools in shaping social imaginary, experiences, public knowledge, and the ways visitors and locals act upon the environment and one another. Just as the big song is inseparable from the eco-sphere that nurtures it, the transformation of the physical environment in Longxing is also intertwined with the change in local social knowledge. The Kam environmental values are increasingly articulated through commercialized development agendas. Despite the 'greening' of the state as evidenced by the passing of environmental laws (Newton & Franklin, 2011), environmental discourse in ethnic rural countryside highlights areas of tensions in reconciling economic growth and ecological sustainability. Place-based education provides an inspiring and meaningful contextual setting for diverse learners (not just students in classrooms) to engage with dialogic exploration of the world and gain critical awareness of social hierarchy and power dynamics therein.

In rural communities such as Longxing, ecotourism promotes two attractions to visitors: firstly, a natural, pristine environment featuring terraced rice fields, vernacular architecture, colorful ethnic costumes, and the general visual effect of timelessness and exoticness; secondly, original customs and lifeways in the village (such as big song singing) that makes the place a cultural type and an appeal in the marketplace. Yet, as the above analysis has shown, the infiltration of tourism industry has produced conflicting environmental changes in Longxing both physically and symbolically. Physically, the purpose of 'looking good' ('worthy of being seen') has heightened spatial control and alteration of the rural landscape, often to the locals' dismay. Symbolically, ethnic singing is packaged as a signature Kam entertainment in the booming tourism industry, while the rich folk ecological understandings distilled in songs are increasingly tokenized and diluted in commercialized tourism agendas.

Thus, the pedagogical functions of ethnic tourism and the big song, as occurring at a particular socioeconomic juncture of China today, produce a form of *subtractive* learning, framing the rural ecology in terms of performative values and entertainment potentials while diminishing the sustaining capacities of folk environmentalism and ecological ethics. The common assumption that rural people are less inclined towards environmental protection compared to their educated urban counterparts (see Harris, 2006; p. 8) is challenged. Bowers (2001) proposes the framework of 'eco-justice' to understand the interconnection between social injustice and the domination of environment, between the subjugation of people in neoliberal economy and the subjugation of lands and ecosystems. In a similar vein, by way of conclusion, I propose a critical pedagogy of place as a means through which rural ethnic Kam people can evaluate their own situations, identify dynamics of social injustice, examine the interactions between development and ecosystems, and articulate their own needs and development trajectories. While ecological concern is largely absent in tourism planning and formal schooling (as they are guided either by profit demands or urban-oriented standardized curricula), a community-engaged, place-based informal education will offer new possibilities to rethink development with ecological ramifications and resituate education within the local context of shared cultural politics.

In recent literature, place-based approach is increasingly associated with environmental, ecological, and rural education (Gruenewald, 2003; Haas & Nachtigal, 1998; Sobel, 1996), emphasizing rural and ecological contexts as informal literacy/curriculum that invites people to critically reflect/act upon their social existence. This echoes Freire's challenge of conventional print-based literacy and redefinition of literacy as place-based, situated experiences through which people encounter the social world. Reading the social processes critically as 'political texts' or 'political curricula' allows social actors to identify, interpret, and transform dominations and neoliberal forces that control how they organize their lives.

A place-based critical pedagogy engages community members to act on their own situationality and interrogate the place and place-making processes. It mobilizes local residents, students, activists, educators, cultural intellectuals to engage in reflexive interpreting of the disruptive neoliberal penetration and remaking of the experiences through localized social action. Giroux and Simon (1989) remind us that events and experiences are not fixed texts passively consumed by learners. Similarly, corporate-produced tourism culture in the Kam community is not a fixed text, but a two-way process in which the local agents themselves can become meaningful co-contributors to the public pedagogy. Given the oral tradition of the Kam community, storytelling can be a powerful counter-pedagogy to inform the public of the ways neoliberal development agenda undermines the community's capacity to define their own environment and brings structural injuries to people's place of dwelling and traditional environmentalism. Even though a difficult proposition in China's instrumental development rationality, a critical pedagogy of place provides a hopeful counternarrative and injects a sense of ecological care and rootedness to the technocratic, economistic conceptions of rural environment.

Disclosure statement

No potential conflict of interest was reported by the author.

Funding

This work was supported by The Social Science Research Council.

Notes

1. See Wong (2014).
2. 'Indigenous' is a politically contentious concept in China. The Chinese government believes the indigenous question is a product of European colonialism, associated with discrimination, oppression, and exploitation, therefore not applicable to the Chinese context. While prohibiting the term *indigenous*, China's 1956 ethnic identification campaign has produced 56 officially recognized ethnic nationalities who live under the development tutelage of the party state. The dominant majority Han accounts for over 92% of the total population, while the 55 minority groups make up the remaining 8%. See Sturgeon, 2007.
3. Autonomy is of course a relative term in Chinese social political context. As tourism planning in Qiandongnan is taken over by external developers, and ethnic singing/dancing increasingly choreographed by urban experts rather than local artists, the limited sense of local autonomy is further truncated.
4. Pseudonym.
5. Although the findings are more appropriately contextualized to the locality, and generalizability is not usually intended in ethnographic works, Geertz's famous dictum well summarizes the ethnographic merit that 'anthropologists don't study villages ... they study *in* villages' (1973, p. 22). In other words, the in-depth understanding of a specific case

provides a bird's-eye view of issues and phenomena that transcend the geographic boundaries of the research field site and orient towards broader cultural theses. See Geertz, C. (1973). *The interpretation of culture*. New York: Basic Books.

6. 'One Conference Two Festivals' refer to the commemoration of the 75th anniversary of the Liping Conference held by the Political Bureau of the Chinese Communist Party during the Long March and the 23rd anniversary of the then President Hu Jintao's speech at the Academic Seminar of the Liping Conference, as well as the celebration of the 4th Kaili Ethnic Cultural Festival and the 3rd Liping Drum Tower Cultural Festival in 2009. Such grand production of festive commemoration is typical of China's statecraft and its visuality driven political climate.
7. The sense of culpability is stated gravely in a letter distributed by the village government to Longxingers: 'An important opportunity has arrived for our village to change its fate by turning into a reputable tourism destination. If you fail to participate and cooperate, you will become historical wrongdoers of the village.'
8. From *ga wang* (songs about the emperor), a big song category in Salong village. See Ingram, 2011, p. 446.
9. The land requisition price in Longxing in 2010 was twenty-four thousand yuan (400 USD) per *mu*. *Mu* is the customary Chinese unit of measurement for area, and the conversion to acre is roughly calculated at 1 acre = 6 *mu*.
10. The lament about the loss of lands as a deeply felt personal and communal crisis is also documented elsewhere in nonindustrial societies where incipient capitalism mediates feelings of anxiety and extends land dispossession to psychological problems and moral disorder (see Geissler & Prince, 2010).
11. Local farmers who refused to give up their lands were criticized for being short-sighted and jeopardizing the future of the village development.
12. The Kam language belongs to the Tai-Kadai family and is divided into two major dialect groupings: the Southern Kam and the Northern Kam.
13. See Ingram, 2011, p. 447.
14. In minority villages such as Longxing, teaching in lower grades of primary school often entails mixed usage of the ethnic language and Mandarin Chinese to help children transition from the mother tongue-only living environment to official language of the schools. The language of instruction gradually shifts to Mandarin only in later years of primary school and beyond.

References

Armstrong, P. (2005). The Simpsons and democracy: Political apathy, popular culture, and lifelong learning as satire. In R. Hill & R. Kiely (Eds.), *Proceedings of the 46th Annual Adult Education Research Conference* (pp. 7–12). Athens: University of Georgia.

Bowers, C. A. (2001). *Educating for eco-justice and community*. Athens: The University of Georgia Press.

Bryman, A. (2004). *The Disneyization of society*. Thousand Oaks, CA: Sage.

Chio, J. T. (2014). *Landscape of travel: The work of tourism in rural ethnic China*. Seattle, WA: University of Washington Press.

Compulsory Education Law of the People's Republic of China. 1986. Retrieved from http://www.china.org.cn/government/laws/2007-04/17/content_1207402.htm

Cornet, C. (2009). Ethnic tourism development: Preliminary data for the Dong village of Zhaoxing, China. In H. Cao (Ed.), *Ethnic minorities and regional development in Asia: Reality and challenge* (pp. 193–203). Amsterdam University Press.

Cornet, C. (2012). *The indigenization of tourism-led modernization: The Dong of Zhaoxing, Southeast Guizhou, China (1990–2010)* (Unpublished dissertation). Université Laval, Québec.

Dewey, J. (1938). *Experience and education*. New York, NY: MacMillan.

Dorfman, A., & Mattelart, A. (1975). *How to read Donald Duck: Imperialist ideology in the Disney comic*. New York, NY: International General.

Freire, P. (1995). *Pedagogy of the oppressed*. New York, NY: Continuum. (Original work published 1970).

Geertz, C. (1973). *The interpretation of culture*. New York, NY: Basic Books.

Geissler, P. W., & Prince, R. J. (2010). *The land is dying: Contingency, creativity and conflict in Western Kenya*. New York, NY: Berghahn Books.

Giroux, H. (1988). *Teachers as intellectuals: Toward a critical pedagogy of learning*. South Hadley, MA: Bergin Garvey.

Giroux, H. (2004). Public pedagogy and the politics of neoliberalism: Making the political more pedagogical. *Policy Futures in Education, 2*, 494–503.

Giroux, H., & Simon, R. I. (Eds.). (1989). *Popular culture, schooling, and everyday Life*. New York, NY: Bergin & Garvey.

Gruenewald, D. A. (2003). The best of both worlds: A critical pedagogy of place. *Educational Researcher, 32*, 3–12.

Haas, T., & Nachtigal, P. (1998). *Place value*. Charleston, WV: ERIC Press.

Harris, P. G. (2006). Environmental perspectives and behavior in China: Synopsis and bibliography. *Environment and Behavior, 38*, 5–21.

Ingram, C. (2011). Echoing the environment in Kam big song. *Asian Studies Review, 35*, 439–455.

Ingram, C. (2012). Tradition and divergence in Southwestern China: Kam big song singing in the village and on stage. *The Asia Pacific Journal of Anthropology, 13*, 434–453.

Luo, H. (2010). Lun dongzu dage de lishi yanjin ji renwen shengtai baohu (论侗族大歌的历史演进及人文生态保护). *Yinyue chuangzuo (音乐创作), 3*, 126–127.

Min, Q., & Zhang, D. (2008). Ecological connotation of some Dong minority taboos (侗族禁忌文化的生态学解读). *Geographical Research (地理研究), 27*, 1437–1443.

Newton, J., & Franklin, A. (2011). Delivering sustainable communities in China: Using a sustainable livelihoods framework for reviewing the promotion of 'ecotourism' in Anji. *Local Environment, 16*, 780–806.

Nyíri, P. (2006). *Scenic spots: Chinese tourism, the state, and cultural authority*. Seattle, WA: University of Washington Press.

Oakes, T. (1998). *Tourism and modernity in China*. New York, NY: Routledge.

Oakes, T. (2006). The village as theme park: Mimesis and authenticity in Chinese tourism. In T. Oakes & L. Schein (Eds.), *Translocal China: Linkages, identities, and the reimagining of space* (pp. 166–192). London: Routledge.

Pan, G. P. (1999). Energizing China: Reconciling environmental protection and economic growth (review). *China Review International, 6*, 497–503.

Sandlin, J. A., & Milam, J. L. (2008). 'Mixing pop (culture) and politics': Cultural resistance, cultural jamming, and anti-consumption activism as critical public pedagogy. *Curriculum Inquiry, 38*, 323–350.

Schein, L. (2000). *Minority rules: The Miao and the feminine in China's cultural politics*. Durham, NC: Duke university Press.

Scott, J. (2009). *The art of not being governed: An anarchist history of upland Southeast Asia*. New Haven, NJ: Yale University Press.

Sobel, D. (1996). *Beyond ecophobia: Reclaiming the heart in nature education*. Great Barrington, MA: The Orion Society and The Myrin Institute.

Stanley, N. (1998). *Being ourselves for you: The global display of cultures*. London: Middlesex University Press.

Sturgeon, J. C. (2007). Pathways of 'indigenous knowledge' in Yunnan, China. *Alternatives: Global, Local, Political, 32*, 129–153.

Tisdell, E. J., & Thompson, P. M. (2006). *Crash*-ing into pop culture in dealing with diversity: Adult education and critical media literacy about movies and television. In M. Hagen & E. Goff (Eds.), *Proceedings of the 47th Annual Adult Education Research Conference* (pp. 425–431). Minneapolis, MN: University of Minnesota.

Wong, E. (2014, February 13). China to reward cities and regions making progress on air pollution. *New York Times*.

Wu, B., He, K., Fan, Y., & Zhao, W. (1998). The status and trend of China's policies on climate change. In M. B. McElroy, C. P. Nielson, & P. Lydon (Eds.), *Energizing China: Reconciling environmental protection and economic growth* (pp. 541–554). Harvard: Harvard University Press.

Xinhua Net. 2007. *Shengtai wenming*. Retrieved May 4, 2014, from http://news.xinhuanet.com/politics/2007-11/06/content_7015615.htm

Yang, Z. (2014). *The general outline of China Dong culture exhibition center. Zhaoxing, Liping County, Guizhou Province*. Unpublished, personal communication.

Zhang, Z. X. (2007). China is moving away the pattern of "develop first and then treat the pollution". *Energy Policy, 35*, 3547–3549.

Zhuang, H., Lassoie, J., & Wolf, S. (2011). Ecotourism development in China: Prospects for expanded roles for non-governmental organizations. *Journal of Ecotourism, 10*, 55–72.

Vernadsky meets Yulgok: A non-Western dialog on sustainability

TAMARA SAVELYEVA

Abstract

This article starts by noting the general lack of acknowledgment of alternative traditions in the dominant western sustainability discourse in education. After critically analyzing the western human–nature relationship in the context of Enlightenment, modernity and colonial expansion, this article introduces two non-western ecological discourses from Eurasia and Asia, Noösphærism and Neo-Confucianism, which offer clear contrasts to the western sustainability framework. Using theoretical argumentations, the article goes on to examine the cosmological and ontological categories expounded by Vladimir Vernadsky of Russia and Yulgok Yi of Korea, whose philosophical foundations with unique foci on the anthropocosmic and cosmoanthropic types of human–nature relationships could well be alternatives and/or additions to the dominant western discourse. The article concludes with a twofold comparison: between Eurasian and Confucian heritages, and these two with the mainstream western ecological discourse.

The majority of researchers and their investigations on sustainability in education belong to the western ecological tradition. This comes as no surprise, since sustainability as social discourse, action philosophy, and movement can all be traced back to the West (Capra, 1997; Norgaard, 1994; Savelyeva & Park, 2012). As if as a result, sustainability education researchers tend to focus on the implementation of the related policies in both western and non-western societies regardless of the cultural and geographical contexts of different sustainability-related traditions. It is needless to say that western sustainability as a whole is regarded as a hegemonic discourse, which often neglects those traditions that originated outside western borders.

Such a neglect of local and regional sustainability traditions by western scholars is perhaps the most critical entropy of the dominant western discourse and this trend can clearly be seen in education. Educational philosophers and researchers in the field have generally fallen short of acknowledging alternative non-western perspectives to be a

This article was originally published with errors. This version has been amended. Corrigendum (http://dx.doi.org/10.1080/00131857.2016.1216638).

significant factor in shaping sustainability education. Instead, energy and resources have been devoted to corroborate what does and what does not work, as well as in permanent searches for best practices, and successful and not so successful policy implementations.

Such trends have extended their influence on Asia and Eurasia through modernization first; recently they have continued under an umbrella of globalization. At the same time, international sustainability policy implementation has been criticized for using exclusively socioeconomic and political parameters that led it to be tagged as the new grand narrative replacing modernism or a new fundamentalism of its own right (NAS, 2015). The phenomenon calls for alternative ecological and ontological categories, which in turn might inform global citizens with contextually resonating and culturally sensitive sustainability discourses.

To respond to this call for alternatives, in this paper I introduce, analyze, and connect two non-western traditions, namely Russian noöspherism and Korean neo-Confucianism. Unlike other native traditions (e.g. Amazonian or Chinese animism), noöspherism and neo-Confucianism are based on actual philosophical works of two scholars—Vladimir Vernadsky and Yi Yulgok. Their works include ontological and epistemological categories, which offer a helpful contrast to the dominant western sustainability discourse. A major point of difference between these two discourses and the West is the ontology of natural relationships, such as human positions concerning nature and other beings, as well as a scale of ecological arguments.

In describing the neo-Confucian and noöspheric ontological categories which are based on cosmoanthropic and anthropocosmic human–nature relationships, I argue that these ontologies shape different perceptions, worldviews, and cultures of Asia and Eurasia. Affected by modernity and colonization, they remain true to their own traditions, relating to cosmos, rather than nature and treating cosmos as a living and dynamic entity, which is interpreted by human ability to envision and be interacted upon. Before discussing these traditions, it is necessary to reflect on the origin and characteristics of western sustainability discourse, as well as possible reasons for its weakening discursive power.

Ecological Discourse in the West

Originated outside academic environs and research offices, sustainability has been closely identified with education for the last three decades. The history of its ascent includes the birth of a field, a new social discourse at the international level, and the reports/recommendations by international agencies with directions to introduce a sustainability agenda into the educational systems.

Sustainability discourse can be traced back to the birth of ecology as a scientific field of studies in the early 1960s. At that time, ecology answered the social demand for addressing environmental disasters and social concerns, associated with human relationship to Earth. Ecology was popularized through literary and policy channels (e.g. Rachel Carson's novel *Silent Spring* in 1962; *Limits of Growth* report to the Club of Rome by Meadows and others in 1972). Responding to a massive wave of public concern, several intergovernmental meetings and the United Nations hosted summits clarifying the terms of sustainability discourse and articulating its key tenets for different educational systems in the world.

Despite decades of international 'reorientation toward sustainability' (Sterling, 2001, p. 17), the sustainability education discourse has rarely been perceived as a rigorous scholarly field (Savelyeva, 2012, 2013). Originated in the West, it has largely been regarded as a fast evolving action-oriented plan tied up to corresponding international and national agendas. Accordingly, the implementation of 'ecological education' was guided by a report of the 1978 intergovernmental meeting in Tbilisi. 'Ecological education' was superseded by the 'environmental education' articulated in the famous report Agenda 21 Chapter 36 of the UN summit in Rio de Janeiro in 1992. After the Rio+ 10 World Summit on Sustainable Development in Johannesburg, the motto became 'sustainability education'[1] and it became officially used in the educational policies and practices worldwide.

Over the years, sustainability-related research in education has produced a large body of literature on educational implementation, successes, challenges, and effects of the global agenda, campaigns, curricular changes, greening investment and action, presented at different levels of perceptions and operational understandings. The ensuing great expansion in related research also indicates that, despite all these efforts, sustainability education has only achieved meager results.

It was reported that sustainability education programs, initiatives, and curricula, both formal and non-formal, generally made no much difference in societal views, attitudes, and behaviors concerning nature or sustainability issues (Bell & Morse, 1999; Chawla, 1998; Hines, Hungerford, & Tomera, 1986; Kollmuss & Agyeman, 2002; Sterling, 2001). One reason that researchers pointed to was that sustainability has been treated as an objective and measurable change in education rather than an emergent entity (Bell & Morse, 1999). Its educational agendas were quantified and loaded with sustainability indicators that have added to sustainability implementation and further challenges, and set the huge goal of 'creating the new patterns of behavior of individual, groups, and societies as a whole toward the environment' (UNESCO-UNEP, 1978).

It was soon realized that beyond the technicalities of sustainability measurements lies the 'most blatant challenge of modernity' (Norgaard, 1994). Modernity might also underlie other reasons often cited for the lack of a significant progress, such as the marginalized status of sustainability education, as well as the absence of interest to sustainability education from governments that, in the words of the previous UNESCO director-general Matsuura, 'view sustainability education like a burden while adjusting to the demands of global competition' (cited in Sterling, 2001, p. 36).

The key categories of the western sustainability discourse include ideas of relation, change, and action, which are rooted in the western modernity. They can be translated into the following goals of sustainability education: (1) to improve human social, environmental, and economic relationships; (2) to transform the existing paradigm of education; and (3) to nurture sustainable and responsible behavior. These categories derive from a western worldview stemmed from modernity and Enlightenment; the topic has been explored by many authors of sustainability (Berman, 1981; Capra, 1997; Norgaard, 1994; Sterling, 2003).

During the Enlightenment, the idea of human separation from and superiority over nature took its current form. A theoretical breakthrough in the western understanding of human relationship with nature came from a notion of anthropomorphism as an expression of human–nature proximity. Within this view, works of René Descartes and Louis Buffon are of particular importance, as they set a stage for the development of western natural science. Descartes's thesis of mind–body duality grounded western thought in a permanent separation from nature for the coming centuries of scientific discoveries. Berger (2009) commented on the Descartes' *Discours de la méthod* (1637) as a breaking point in the western understanding of the relationship to nature:

> Descartes internalized, *within man*, the dualism implicit in the human relation to animals. In deriving absolutely body from soul, he bequeathed the body to the laws of physics and mechanics, and since animals were soulless, the animal was reduced to the model of a soulless machine. (2009, p. 13)

The influence of Descartes is clearly reflected in the works of the noted French naturalist Louis Buffon, remembered by his encyclopedic work on natural history *Histoire naturelle, générale et particulière.* In his chapter on beavers, for example, Buffon clearly pointed to the man-to-nature divide: 'in proportion as man rises above a state of nature, the other animals sink below that standard. [They are] reduced to slavery, or treated as rebels, and dispersed by force' (cited in Moran, n.d.).

Enlightenment inspired modern science and vice versa. Its cultural legacy includes mechanistic ontologies, primary materialism and determinism, and epistemologies built on objectivism, reductionism, positivism, and dualism. They became a permanent expression of the western cultural paradigm, which embedded ideas of development and progress at the expense of nature. When later on, European nation–states added a new political element of colonial expansion to the ideas of modernity, a massive territorial occupation and exploitation of nature was justified and reified. In their race for supremacy in war and colonization, the nation–states 'organized and reaped some of the fruits of the "discovery" and exploitation of non-European lands as it became essential to equip, plan and finance exploration, and manage newly acquired posts and territories' (Held, 1992, p. 99). Therefore, territorial occupation driven by the idea of West-led modernization was and perhaps still is a major legacy and source of unsustainability and environmental degradation (Park, 2016).

The consequences of western colonization and impacts of modernity on non-western school of thoughts are alive and visible. On the one hand, there is an 'Asia and the rest' framework proposed by the Taiwanese scholar Kuan-Hsing Chen (2010), who provided a unique account of Asia's knowledge structure, social dynamics, and decolonization at odds with the western knowledge production (K.H. Chen, personal conversation, July 4, 2013). According to Chen (2010), a new form of imperialism is in the heart of post-colonial Asia:

> Capital-driven forces seek to penetrate and colonize all spaces on the earth with unchecked freedom, and that in so doing have eroded national frontiers and integrated previously unconnected zones. In this ongoing process of globalization, unequal power relations become intensified, and imperialism expresses itself in a new form. (p. 4)

The idea that South-East Asian societies were quite modern (and, perhaps, sustainable) thousands of years before the arrival of imperialism and, that they adapted new ideas from outside for a thousand years to come is evident from the replacement of the term *pre-colonial* with *early modern*. *Early modernity* in South-East Asia, as a historical period and a concept, involves a sense of separation from local tradition: the West brought in promises of power, growth, and transformation, at the same time threatening to destroy the founding postulates of 'the rest' (Berman, 1982). In the words of Barbara Andaya (1997),

> [Modernity was] slowly robbing the past of its authority to direct the shape of the present … Not only did respect for the learning of the Ancients seep away; their teachings could even become a source of derision. 'How was it,' asked one sceptic, 'that men were attracted to tales so manifestly absurd?' (p. 394)

Built up on a sense of separateness and a lack of attention to alternative worldviews, ontological categories, and traditions, western modernity is associated with distortion and inherent instability (Berman, 1981) related to a separation of humans and nature. In search for the alternatives, Berman calls for a reversal of human perceptions, which would 're-enchant' the world from the consequences of modernity with more holistic and participating worldviews and social structures:

> The crux of modern dilemma [is that] we cannot go back to alchemy or animism—at least that does not seem likely, but the alternative is grim, scientific, totally controlled world of nuclear reactors, micro processing, and genetic engineering—the world which is virtually upon as already. *Some* type of holistic or participating consciousness and a corresponding sociopolitical formation have to emerge if we are to survive as species. (p. 23)

The above discussion indicates that western views of sustainability narrow the contemporary understandings of what might constitute sustainability beyond the eastern borders of Europe, as they dismiss the non-western, perhaps, more authentic frameworks and traditions.

However, while non-western discussions of sustainability have been tied up to the concepts of modernity and colonialism, western scholars moved the entire discussion to the area of postmodernity, starting a revision of key western assumptions 'stemming from long-held traditions associated with the modern western worldview' (Sterling, 2003, p. 198). In this sense, attention to the non-western ontologies fits into this emerging postmodern direction in the field, as it helps to identify different conceptual flows and alternatives. Such identifications might pull sustainability discourse to a whole new level by engaging new views that rarely, if at all, interchanged boundaries with western notions of sustainability in the past.

The postmodern perspectives in sustainability discourse bring out its focus on change, powers, participation, resistance, and so on. In this view, education could be seen as a tool for implementing change toward a more sustainable world in both social and cultural contexts. However, these contexts often assign to education a role of mere socialization and preservation of traditions and knowledge, rather than transformation. This creates a structural trap (Savelyeva, 2012) for implementing sustainability in educational systems. Sterling (2003) suggested that, from a perspective of critical theory, these paradoxes have resulted from the social need to keep hegemony, when the dominant educational paradigm limits the alternative forms that promote change.

Eurasian Noöspherism of Vernadsky

Just across the eastern borders of Europe, the Russian philosopher of science Vladimir Vernadsky (1945) came up with a novel idea of *noösphere* (from Greek νος—mind and σφαρα—sphere) in or before 1926. A globalist and a founding father of biogeochemistry, Vernadsky was also a child of Enlightenment and modernity. However, unlike most of the intellectuals and scientists of his time, his main understanding and approach to the human–nature relationship was quite different.

The idea of *noösphere* or 'thinking stratum' emerged during Vernadsky's tenure at the Sorbonne University in the early 1920s, in discussion with Pierre Teilhard de Chardin and Édouard Le Roy, who attended Vernadsky's lectures on geochemistry. Although never explicitly defining it, Vernadsky refers to *noösphere* in his seminal work *The Biosphere* (1926/1998) as the final stage of Earth's evolution driven by powers of interconnected human minds. It is important to mention that the idea of *noösphere* was later taken on board by Teilhard (1955/1959), a theologian and Jesuit priest, who developed his own interpretation of the term and popularized it during his work in the then newly established UNESCO.

Although Teilhard's concept of *noösphere* was before the emergence of the terms 'ecology' and 'sustainability,' it was significantly different from the Vernadskian's version. In his discussion on *noösphere*, Teilhard cultivated its social and spiritual aspects, arguing that *noösphere* will evolve humanity to the 'Omega Point,' an apex of thought as per noogenesis, with love being its principal driver. In this sense, Teilhard's idea of *noösphere* remained anthropocentric, keeping the human–nature relationship in dominance of the former.

In contrast, Vernadskian's *noösphere* was anthropocosmic. Although humans were still featured as an important evolutionary force, their relationship with the universe, rather than natural environment of the Earth, was a major point of departure. As the last evolutionary stage of the *biosphere*,[2] a term which was also coined for science by Vernadsky (1938/2012), *noösphere* was a purely scientific notion:

> Considering such a condition of our knowledge, we can distinguish an expression of the influence on the structure of the noösphere of two areas of human thought: the sciences common to all reality (physics, astronomy,

> chemistry, mathematics), and sciences related to the Earth (biological, geological, and humanistic sciences). (p. 31)

This pioneering conceptualization was rooted in his philosophy of science and foundations of Eurasian cosmological thought. The three distinctive aspects of Vernadskian's *noösphere* that relate the theory to the western sustainability movement are: (1) anthropocosmic ontological views on human–nature relationship; (2) planetary scale of argument[3] founded in the Eurasian cosmism, and (3) critical role of human thought over action in the evolution of the planet.

Spiritual origins of the Vernadskian notion of *noösphere* are emphasized in the role of emotional experience or feelings he assigns to human beings in a process of acquiring the noöspheric stage of earth evolution. Comparing Vernadskian emotion with a state of Einstein's 'cosmic religious feeling,' Mochalov (1988) summarized it as an 'emotional experience of unity with living nature, with cosmos in general, with living nature in particular, sense of cosmic nature of life and mind, and harmony of the universe' (p. 68).

According to the principles of Eurasian cosmism, the origin of human beings and human consciousness belongs to the depth of cosmos. Cosmos within noöspherism is viewed as a combination of both physical and natural states of all living beings, where earth is considered as a living and evolving being by itself. A principle of eternality of life and unity of life forms is essential to cosmism. Formulated by Vernadsky, in his seminal work on synthesis of cosmos, a cosmic feature of the living matters is one of the main factors of noöspheric evolution: 'phenomena of life allow one to investigate cosmos beyond [human] comprehension, so far impossible by any known means. This is a manifestation of cosmic nature of life' (Vernadsky, 1926/1998, p. 273).

Vernadskian cosmology combines a scientific approach to investigations of planetary phenomena with the philosophical means of inquiry, putting humans' 'thinking strata' in the center of geological and spiritual affairs. Thus, cosmos might be approached as an object and a subject for the purpose of explaining metaphysical matters of life and living universe. Despite its obvious appeal to western scientific tradition, Eurasian cosmism is unique as it uses holistic approaches and symbolic interpretations. It is also different from the western understanding of cosmos:

> in Russian cosmism, a universal being, an entire existence of life serves as a symbol of unity of all living forms. Universe is life, in all its diversity of forms, on earth and beyond earth. If for Enlightenment thinkers nature was an entity separated from cosmos, for Russian cosmists, the universe appeared as a single living organism, inseparable from nature. (Usoltsev, 2010, p. 45)

As one of the influential figures of the late stream in the Russian philosophical school of cosmism, Vernadsky (1938/2012) argued that the evolutionary motion of the biosphere to its final noöspheric stage might be set forward by humans' 'thinking strata' and guided by scientific reasoning. Vernadsky described *noösphere* as a new form of biogeochemical energy that affects the most important characteristic of the biosphere, life. He referred to this energy as the energy of human culture or cultural biogeochemical energy, which has manifested only recently:

> Its manifestation in the predecessors of Man was probably developed over the course of hundreds of millions of years, but it was able to express itself as a geological force only in our time, when Homo sapiens has embraced the entire biosphere with his life and cultural work. (p. 18)

Attention to human intellectual and spiritual power as a driving force of planetary evolution allows the noöspheric theory to enter social dimensions of human affairs, particularly, through the developments of science. Within the noöspheric theory, science is considered as more of a natural phenomenon than a social institution. Thus, the process of evolving into the new evolutionary stage as a scientific phenomenon is inextricable and without pause:

> The noösphere reworked by scientific thought is produced by a process that took place during millions, perhaps billions of years to create *homo sapiens faber,* is not a short-term transient ecological phenomenon. Processes which take billions of years cannot cease. Consequently, biosphere will transform into noösphere, one way or another, sooner or later. In the history of those who populate it, the events necessary for this transformation, will happen and they cannot be contradicted. (Vernadsky, 1926/1998)

A relevant question to follow is about the implications of scientific thought on noöspheric developments in terms of values and actions. For Usoltsev (2010), Vernadsky took the idea of life and cosmos as integrating principles of the world and also emphasized that the universe and humans have their mutual coresponses through the evolutionary movement from biosphere to *noösphere*. Vernadsky had a belief that the scientific developments will strengthen human sense of unity and responsibility by gradually expanding human understanding of cosmic ontologies.

In noöspheric tradition, the most important human relationships are those that concern the universe at a cosmic scale of affairs rather than being reduced to human affairs. This allows us to reasonably conclude that Vernadskian's noöspherism is a rich resource of inspiration for developing noöspherology *qua* field of study (Akimov, 2013), a discipline that integrates all scientific dimensions under the umbrella of noöspheric theory, which emphasizes the role of human reason in evolution of the entire planet.

Neo-Confucianism of Yulgok

Father to the East, Yi-Yi (李珥), the most renowned Korean neo-Confucian scholar, known by the penname Yulgok, offers a different understanding of the human–nature relationship in the late sixteenth century. His *Bu* (賦 ode) on *Yi-il-boon-soo* (理一分殊 One Principle, Different Parts) gives a poetic account of cosmic ontology, with a starting argument that cosmos was originally one and, once divided, each part of it retained a unique form or characteristic (1814/1968).

In Yulgok's neo-Confucian thought, Tae-geuk (太極 cosmos or universe), is the origin of all things and a foundational state prior to the differentiation between Heaven and Earth. The Earth is understood in relation to the universe and it is expressed as a dual concept 'Heaven and Earth,' where humans are positioned in harmony with Heaven. This relationship is expressed in the Confucian term of 'making one with Heaven and the human,' which is a process that could be achieved through individual self-cultivation. Yulgok's ontology is cosmoanthropic, as it positions Tae-geuk or cosmos at the center of all affairs concerning living matters, including humans.

This cosmoanthropic vision is different from a classic anthropocosmic Confucianism approach to cosmology (Tu, 2001). The difference between the two lies in the direction of the relationship between humans and the Tae-geuk. According to Yulgok, the unity of human and Tae-geuk, Heaven and Earth, starts with and is governed by the cosmic flows. In contrast, the classic anthropocosmic Confucianism puts humans in the center of cosmic affairs and explains the ontological unity from a standpoint of humans reaching out to the universe and wisdom through a process of self-cultivation. Yulgok's cosmoanthropic view implies focus on the universe as a starting point for the fundamental *Eum* (陰)—*Yang* (陽) (*Ying-Yang* in Chinese pronunciation) that generates, transforms, and harmonizes all living beings in the universe.

In his *Treatise on the Way to Heaven* (天道策), Yulgok explains in detail how *Eum-Yang* rules the unity of humans and the universe with the dynamic principle of *li-qi*, its vital force, which is inherent in the cosmos. Yulgok's (1814/1968, Book 1, Ode) ontological categories are both poetic and metaphoric in style:

> Eum (陰) has rooted in the movement and Yang (陽) is in the quiet. If the move and the quiet became one, who divided it into Heaven and Earth? Yellowish square shaped Earth to become the foundation; obscure gas started in Heaven. If the effects of Heaven and Earth are different, then, who has threaded it through turning them into one? It is a mystery because it is one; they are two then they change things. There are odd things inside hollow things; nothingness is stuck inside something. The Way (道) is not outside form; the principle coexists with material things. Change is infinite and water stream, restless. Who did take care of such a system? Oh, Tae-geuk (太極) it is.

To this almost magical, yet clearly dualistic elaboration on the origin and nature of the cosmos, Yulgok appends a poem (詩) with a related story. One day, Yulgok was sightseeing the Phong-hak Mountains and came across a small hermitage, where a Buddhist monk was meditating alone. He noticed that the kitchen has not been used for days and asked the monk, 'What do you eat?' The monk pointed at a pine tree implying that he was getting nurture from the tree's skin. Yulgok playfully challenged the monk, 'Who is more saint (聖人), Buddha or Confucius?' The monk answered with a smile, 'Do not tease an old monk'. Their ensuing dialog reaches a critical moment with the following thought experiment (1814/1968], Book 1, Poetry):

> I told him 'There is a saying "Kite flies to the sky and fish is jumping in the pond." Is this color or nothingness?' The monk said 'It is neither color nor

> nothingness. It is a foundational form of the principle of balance, so how can we possibly understand it through poetry?' With a mirth, I said, 'If there are words, it means that they are already delimited, so how could we possibly say that it is a foundational form? If that is the case, while Confucianism's wonders cannot be transmitted with words, the way of Buddha would be a mere set of written letters'.

At this, the monk became very impressed and said, 'You are not an ordinary scholar. Please tell me and explain the point'. Yulgok wrote a poem and handed it over to the monk, who having read it, turned his back again to face the wall to mediate. Three days later, Yulgok went back to see the monk, but he found only the shaft with the monk gone.

The issue calls for further exploration. Only one more written work contains explicit discussion on Tae-geuk (太極). The book nine of his *Complete Works* (1814/1968) comprises three letters, which Yulgok wrote to Park Hwa Suk, a powerful politician and literati of Korea at that time. A reference to Tae-geuk appears in the second letter:

> Confucius said in the text of Joo-yeuk(周易) [Zhou Yi in Chinese] that *Tae-geuk* has given origin to *Eum* and *Yang*. Also, Zhou-ji (周子) in Joo-donni said, 'It is endless and *Tae*geuk is all at once.' I am not sure therefore why Your Lordship considers all these as something happened after the creation of heaven and earth? You asked me whether *Tae-geuk* is independently hanging in the air. It is not so. A theory that supports the [concept of] foundation only says, '*Tae-geuk* is the foundation of *Eum* and *Yang*. There has never been a time when *Tae-geuk* is separated from *Eum* and *Yang*.'

There are another five references to Tae-geuk in the third letter, where Yulgok refutes prima facie a claim that Tae-geuk gives birth to Eum and Yang. Yulgok calls this idea, arguing that Eum-Yang is an ever existing entity, which was not generated at a given moment. One might find his refutation categorical, yet, Yulgok elaborated on his stance in the latter part of the same letter:

> When *Eum* is done, *Yang* appears; *Yang* is over, then *Eum* appears … *Tae-geuk* is elsewhere either *Eum* or *Yang*. This is the reason why *Tae-geuk* is the pivot and node of countless changes and the foundation of all existing things.

Here, Yulgok offers a counter argument to the idea that Eum and Yang generated: 'If there is a start, there should be a final annihilation. If so, the principle of Eum and Yang would have ended long ago. How could this be plausible?'

Yulgok's argumentation on the matters of Eum and Yang reveals his hermeneutics of cosmos, which includes the emphasis on a cosmic centrality and order, notion of ever existence and dynamics of life, and respect for life and its processes. These ideas might be paralleled with the Vernadskian notion of *Biosphere*, where life, as a non-naturalistic phenomenon, has being as its central characteristic. Both Yulgok and

Vernadsky do not use the term 'nature' opposite to 'humans.' For Vernadsky, 'nature' equals 'universe,' and Yulgok relates to the hierarchies of Heaven and Earth to describe the structure of the universe, without referring to 'nature' in his explanatory narratives.

Comparable categories might also be found among western thinkers, such as Albert Schweitzer's ethics of reverence for life, that clearly resonate with the principle of respect to universal processes featured in Yulgok's books. Relevant today, Yulgok's cosmoanthropic approach to the human–universe relationship and an assumption that everything in the universe, including humans, shares life and deserves greatest respect has singled him out of the classic stream of Confucian thought at his time. A symbolic structure of Yulgok's universe, which he understood as an open and organized system, where everything—every living being and the universe itself—reflects on its rules, dynamics, and principles and is governed by them, brings out a notion of reality open to endless possibilities and variations. This can be paralleled with the relatively recent works of western quantum physics and a corresponding stream of systematism in western social sciences.

Confucian ecological thoughts have been propagating in the West, arguably, since the 1996 'Confucianism and Ecology' conference held at Harvard University. During almost 20 years of scholarship, a body of literature on this topic has been gradually increasing, albeit it remains limited mostly to the area of religious philosophy and Asian studies. The researchers in this area mainly focus on reviewing anthropocentric tendencies in the classic Confucian texts (Tu, 2001), describing distinct ecological features from the perspective of cosmology (Ro, 2011) and environmental ethics (He, 2000; Shi, 2007). The scholars also discuss the differences between various ancient classic and neo-Confucius ideas in relation to the western eco-philosophy (Zheng, 2010). It is generally agreed that although both classic and neo-Confucianism contain ecological characteristics, they are 'originally not a philosophy that was established on an ecological foundation' (Hon, 2011, p. 33).

Discussion: Vernadsky meets Yulgok

My choice of Vernadsky and Yulgok was purposeful, if not arbitrary. The reason for this choice is because the ontologies of these two thinkers provide the most contrasting and unique alternative to the western discourse, which was born in the context of the Pax Americana and Eurocentrism. Truthfully, it is not possible to claim that Yulgok and Vernadsky fully succeeded in reaching out to a global audience with a profound and universal impact on the western philosophy of science. After all, Yulgok was elaborating in the context of the Hermit Kingdom (Yi dynasty Korea) of the sixteenth century, whereas Vernadsky was caught by the political turmoil of the late Russian Empire and Soviet Russia in the early twentieth century. The contributions of Yulgok and Vernadsky should be seen not as a widespread global agenda to replace the dominant western sustainability framework, but as content-rich alternative discourses emerging from local and regional contexts that are clear and distinct from the contemporary philosophy and theory on sustainability.

Comparing the anthropocosmic and cosmoanthropic ideas of Vernadsky and Yulgok might provide an understanding of humanity as a cosmic category. For Yulgok, cosmos is not an object, physical reality, or a mechanical entity; cosmos is a dynamic and ever changing interpretive reality, which reflects human understanding, sense-making and interpretation of the universe. Vernadskian discussion on cosmos is not physical either. Grounded in the philosophy of Russian cosmism (Feodorov, 1906; Roerich, 1923/2009; Solovyev, 1877/1988), Vernadskian universe is one with humans, who need to remain united (from the Russian term соборность (*sobornost*) for the universe to evolve. Vernadsky viewed the universe as a living and evolving entity, which has changed with and by powers of the human mind. Central to the Vernadskian argument was that life and love are the driving forces in the evolutionary process. Human mind—*noös*—plays a pivotal role in science, and science itself cannot be detached from the evolutionary process. Both Yulgok and Vernadsky elaborated a planetary scale argument, many years before the age of space explorations.

Another meeting point of Vernadsky and Yulgok is ontological hierarchies as a category of the human mind. For Yulgok, the universe has a symbolic structure, which humans comprehend through a series of numbers, images, or hexagrams. Humans are, therefore, seen as active agents in this interpretive process. The interpretation, however, requires a certain level of development for person's awareness or perception. Only persons with a developed ability to comprehend universal structure and who are capable of deriving knowledge through interaction with the universe are called sages in Confucian terms. Yulgok names Confucius as one of the true sages who was able to perceive the symbols of the universe through interactions with the cosmic flows. According to Yulgok, the understandings derived from Confucius interactions with the cosmic structures constitute knowledge that the sage passes on to future generations (cited in Ro, 1989):

> Heaven and Earth wait for sages, with numbers, to show [the meaning of the universe] to the world. Sages wait for the clue of written character to show the principle to the world. Heaven has to beget sages; sages have to produce the clue of the written character to show to the world. This is the response of nature and the mutual interaction and mysteries of Heaven and human beings. (p. 6)

This passage challenges the western idea of knowledge and knowing. Sage is not the one who knows all the facts and books, but the one who reads and interprets the symbolic matrix of the universe. Knowledge, therefore, has little to do with the haughty sequence of 'pure *ratio*' and 'supremacy of reason' of the western Enlightenment. Unlike in western science, neo-Confucianism does not consider the human mind to be a central tool in constructing realities. Knowledge becomes a matter of perception and symbolic interpretation. The poem with which Yulgok ends his experiential narrative with the monk (1814/1968, Book 1, Poetry) illustrates the power of symbolic perception:

> Fish jumps and kite flies down and up but in one
> Alas, they are neither color nor nothingness

> After a quite mirth my eyes turn to express gratitude
> only to find the setting sun standing tall in the woods

These rather romantic and naturalist passages might indicate the artistic and human caliber of Yulgok. They could also inspire a reader to explore the main issue at hand, the human–nature (cosmos) relationship. In a conversation with the monk that led to this poem (Book 1), Yulgok argued that language limits the reality: 'if there are words, it means that they are already delimited'. If the phrase 'flying kites' is an articulation of an idea or human mind (*noös*), Yulgok seems to imply that the very utterance of words is an act of delimiting. One way to interpret it with a western outlook is to consider delimitation as an act of determination, including negation, as it was done by Spinoza, a continental philosopher of the seventeenth century (Melamed, 2012; Spinoza, Shirley, Adler, Barbone, & Rice, 1632-1677/1995).

The Vernadskian idea of *noösphere* in its very name holds a message about the importance of reasoning and human perception of the universe:

> With Man, however, the form of biogeochemical energy connected to reason grows and expands with time, rapidly moving to the force. This increase is possibly related to the growth of reason itself—a process which seems to occur very slowly (if at all), but is chiefly connected to its honing and deepening in using it to consciously transform the social environment, and is especially due to the growth of scientific knowledge. (Vernadsky, 1938/2012, p. 18)

He argued that scientific thought as an individual and social phenomenon is inseparable from humans:

> Scientific thought is both individual and social. It is inseparable from Man. Not even in his deepest levels of abstraction can an individual transcend the realm of his existence. Science has a real existence, and like Man himself, is most closely and inextricably bound to the noösphere. The individual is obliterated—'decomposed'—when he goes beyond the logical grasp of his intellect. (p. 31)

The argument about the expansion of a perceptual domain of knowing has also emerged in the western sustainability literature (Bateson, 1980). An example of a new arena of 'perceptual ecology' (Thomashow, 2002), which was launched at the Millennium, has 'open doorways to more holistic and personal experiences that accompany transformative change' (Sterling, 2003, p. 352) to addresses problems of western dualism in a 'biospheric' curricula.

As already noted, the main difference between western and non-western ecological discourses presented here lies in the ontology (hierarchy of beings) of human–nature relationship. The main difference is the western anthropocentric assumption about the natural relationships on the one side, and the anthropocosmic/cosmoanthropic assumptions of Noöspherism and Neo-Confucianism of Yulgok on the other that creates a tension of neglect between the ecological discourses.

This tension of neglect is arguably the main challenge for sustainability education implementation in Asia and Eurasia. The western anthropocentric assumptions that humans are separated from and superior to nature and other living beings, stem from the centuries of western modernity and colonization in these two regions. Such the ontology that sets humans as the main reference point of any natural relationship and assumes human upper hand over directions, responsibilities, and approaches to nature presupposes dialectics of 'human and the rest' followed by a 'supremacy of humans.' As a result, the human mind is innately meant to rule and exploit the rest.

The foregoing is not an exaggeration. It should be noted that this very enlightened anthropocentrism has generated a 'West and the rest' condition of modernity (Chen, 2010; Hall, 1992). The subsequent materialization of modernity discourse has nurtured the ideals of sustainability education as we know it today. Sustainability education is built upon the same underlying assumptions of human dominance at the expense of nature. Thus, it has this sacrosanct imperative of 'development' always lingering around, while the politically correct 'respect for nature' is only insofar 'nature is treated mainly as something that provides useful services to humans' (Dryzek, 2005, p. 156).

Today, the mainstream sustainability education stands on western ecological categories grounded on the anthropocentric conception of the human–nature relationship, where nature needs to be properly managed within the three pillars of sustainability: economy, society, and the environment. Situating these three pillars at the core of any sustainability education policy, curriculum or program has a goal of educating 'green' minds, who are capable of managing nature, its resources, and services in any corner of the world. Thus, sustainability education is largely about social learning and change, and it involves practical, hands-on, and experiential approaches to attain its aim of producing a sustainable person who efficiently manages society, economy, and the environment.

By contrast, noöspherism and neo-Confucianism appear to have far less practical concerns, when they come to education. Regarding human–nature relationships, Vernadskian's anthropocosmism and Yulgok's cosmoanthropism provide bases for a major educational objective to foster a holistic worldview and embed a set of values that allow a harmonious growth of self and society within a larger universe.

A connection between ecological discourses, ideology, and political agendas is unavoidable and it is fair to note that when it comes to a social system, sustainability education considers capitalism by default. All three discourses—sustainability, noöspherism, and neo-Confucianism—have been engaged in politics of corresponding western and non-Western countries in support of the current ideological agendas.

In Russia, Vernadskian ideas of *noösphere* underline a branch of noöspherism that promotes development of the 'noospheric and democratic socialism' (Subetto, 2006, p. 8). To include noöspherism in mainstream Russian education, the discipline of noospherology—intellectual synthesis of all scientific fields on the principles of Vernadskian theory—has been created, included into curriculum, and supported by a recently published textbook for universities.

China's constitution contemplates the country's unique approach to nature, emphasizing 'harmony between man and nature and the principle of all the people building and sharing a harmonious socialist society' (Communist Party of China [CPC], 2007, p. 9). Although it is hard to tell whether this is related to any remnant of ancient Confucian values, what one cannot possibly deny is that China is facing a fast environmental degradation, regardless of its cause. The observed gap between any Confucian value–philosophy and the real life can be explained with a *thin* conception of Confucian heritage that competes neck-and-neck with a *thick* conception of it (Park, 2011).

In the West, the sustainability discourse is not immune to be politicized either. It is argued (NAS, 2015) that sustainability is an ideology[4] that took rather a fundamentalist shape to promote ideas of the Western plutocracy in its attempts to 'unite environmental activism, anti-capitalism, and a progressive vision of social justice' (NAS, 2015, p. 19). Just like practiced by autocratic and totalitarian governments, political responses to sustainability in the West gave the state a right to implement favorable measures, which were justified by a crisis call for fast and sure action.

Despite their political tendencies, all three discourses link themselves to the notion of positive change, which is one of the power ideas for all types of governments in all operating societies. In this respect, the neo-Confucian notion universal of unity and self-cultivation and Vernadskian notion of planetary evolution can be viewed as a common point for engagement or even synergy between the two traditions in the context of social development.

In addition, all three discourses involve rhetoric of reassurance in a dynamic development and change for all (humanity, nature, universe, cosmos, and society). Although unlike western scholars, neo-Confucians and noöspheric scholars view development as an infinite number of possibilities rather than a one-directional way toward social improvement, the rhetoric of reassurance connects the discourses.

At the level of implementation, the insights from these three different discourses provide a rich picture of how one's perception of nature or universe gets transformed into a worldview, which might form an ecological culture. The task of sustainability implementation comes out from the basic assumption of human separation from nature and the dominant position in relation to it. This assumption leads to what Bateson (1972) called an 'epistemological error' of western thought. He argued that the error generates a lapsed circle of errors and leads to a reality, which might develop into a negative loop: 'when you separate mind from the structure in which it is immanent, such as human relationship, the human society, or the ecosystem, you [are led on to] a fundamental error, which in the end will surely hurt you' (p. 461). Contemporary sustainability education might be a showcase when the epistemology of the western discourse 'hurts' its own implementation in Asia and Eurasia by imposing knowledge structures incompatible with the local traditions. With Enlightenment mentality (Tu, 2001), the western epistemologies and ontologies do not fully resonate with the worldviews of non-Westerners, whose mentalities are rooted in the cosmoanthropic and anthropocosmic ontologies and epistemologies.

Furthermore, the Enlightenment project itself as a reductionist paradigm might hinder the process of dialog with cosmoanthropic holists. Neo-Confucian and noöspheric traditions are deeply holistic and systemic, so much so that they acknowledge the intelligence of the universe. In this account, human life and other living matters follow ontologies and functions in a system at the scale of the universe/cosmos. This echoes recent developments in ecological studies that have shifted foci from analytic inquiries to holistic approaches to science, such as complexity, emergence, and spatiality (Delorme, 2010; Page, 2011; Savelyeva & Park, 2012).

Holistic ecological sciences and their approaches note the dynamic connection among different systems at the physical and non-physical levels, emphasizing the complexity of flow of matter, energy, and information. For instance, holism offers an analytical tool to understand a wide range of phenomena (Savelyeva & Park, 2012). To create an account for the engagement among different educational paradigms, Sterling (2003) conceptualized a 'whole system thinking' approach to education. It embraces implementation of systemic views and approaches for a transformation of the educational paradigm and describes the possibility of turning sustainability education into a holistic conceptual model. This model has been implemented in school contexts for about a decade in Australia (Bawden, 2010; Bawden & Reichenbach, 2010), the United Kingdom (Sterling, 2003), Northern Europe (Brunner & Urenje, 2012), and the Americas (Capra, 2003). However, as Sterling (2003) pointed out, Western teachers experience difficulties in teaching and thinking from a whole system perspective. The challenge of implementation makes an in-depth engagement of the whole system thinking with sustainability curricular frameworks fragmented and marginalized (Tilbury & Cooke, 2005). Addressing this situation in classrooms might require a prior change in the dominant education paradigm, which permits and encourages a pedagogical approach that is 'holistic, organismic and ecological' (Sterling, 2003, p. 52).

Conclusion

Since its inception into the education sector, sustainability education has largely been about implementation and benchmarking of ecological ideals in the international arena (Savelyeva & Park, 2012). However, it has also been questioned for its global failure, as well as for imposing western anthropocentrism and its corresponding epistemology upon non-western contexts. While producing and exporting environmental knowledge with western agendas, global sustainability education has largely overlooked non-western traditions. Eurasian anthropocosmism and Asian cosmoanthropism might provide alternative understandings of human–nature relationships and facilitate identifying conceptual drawbacks of the western sustainability education discourse.

In spite of differences in ontology and epistemology (anthropocentric, anthropocosmic, and cosmoanthropic), the discourses of western sustainability, Eurasian noöspherism, and Korean neo-Confucianism have mutual complementary points of engagement. For example, practical and experiential approaches to western sustainability education are quite compatible with the ideologically charged implementations of noöspherism and neo-Confucianism in Eurasian and Asian societies.

These non-western discourses are not at odds with the basic idea of change and growth developed by the western discourse, although the latter might not share political prescriptions of the former. Furthermore, there is no reason to believe that noöspherists and neo-Confucianists will not openly share the holistic and systemic aspects of their teachings with the western sustainability education discourse.

Sustainability theorists have applied these ideas in various ways, including the argument of an educational paradigm shift toward a whole system thinking (Sterling, 2003).

Despite some additive elements, there is also a significant tension between the discourses. One of them is the tension of neglect, when the localized discourses ignore sustainability agendas, while sustainability discourse neglects noöspherism and neo-Confucianism traditions as significant factors for successful implementation. Other tensions relate to the context of these traditions: Noöspherists have key disagreements with a weak stance of sustainable education concerning change and strong anthropocentrism in understanding development. Neo-Confucianists would never agree with Noöspherists about the best way to inquire cosmic matters and humans ordering planetary affairs. One way of easing these tensions would be to admit that different ecological discourses might be applicable to different aspects of ecological issues and educational affairs. In essence, Eurasian noöspheric discourse is about the globalist argument on planetary evolution influenced by human 'thinking stratum'.

Whatever position one might reach in a discussion between other ecological discourses, it would be always possible to follow one of the main threads that constitutes the noöspheric discourse. Another way to use subthreads to find connecting points is by looking at their multilayered and complex structure. For example, one might believe in social change by means of sustainability responsible action (reuse, reduce, and recycle) and, at the same time, believe in a cosmic scale of ecological affairs. These possibilities simply show that each ecological discourse offers a comprehensive account for ecological affairs at all levels, from the global to the local, and across different areas of educational implementation, including politics, social structures, and individual practices.

With these competing and complex examples in mind, I conclude by arguing that ecological discourses, dominant and localized, already constitute and safeguard educational traditions in different countries and geographical regions. Establishing dialog among them demands a major effort. Their noted capacity to facilitate learning and impact social and individual change in their respective educational and cultural contexts might be magnified as they observe each other's limitations as opportunities and become aware of their own shortcomings. In any case, respect and openness to dialog between authentic traditions might lead the localized ecological discourses to implement their own versions of sustainability-oriented education.

Acknowledgments

A special acknowledgment goes to Jae Park for his help with the translation of Yulgok's works and to David Sorrell for his valuable comments. I thank the two anonymous reviewers for their very useful feedback on a script for this article, and the editors for their patience through the long process of revision.

Disclosure statement

No potential conflict of interest was reported by the author.

Funding

This study is a part of the research project entitled *Comparative study of higher education sustainability discourses in Asia and Eurasia* [grant number IELL-MRF-01-2014] supported by Hong Kong Institute of Education.

Notes

1. Following a common practice, I use sustainability education to include the terms education for sustainable development (ESD), education for sustainability (EfS), and education for sustainable future (EFS).
2. Vernadsky viewed biosphere as a single greatest geological force on earth, an equivalent to 'nature' in the ordinary sense of term, a living organism that has been evolving to its final stage by means of living matter and human reasoning.
3. The term 'planetary' refers to the planet Earth as a living and evolving organism.
4. By ideology, NAS implies a self-evident and self-contained doctrine, which presents a set of promises that appear true and important.

References

Akimov, A. K. (2013). *Noöspherology*. Moscow: Ecological Fund of Vernadsky.

Andaya, B. W. (1997). Historicising "modernity" in Southeast Asia. *Journal of the Economic and Social History of the Orient, 40*, 391–409.

Bateson, G. (1972). *Steps to an ecology of mind: Collected essays in anthropology, psychiatry, evolution and epistemology*. London: Paladin Granada.

Bateson, G. (1980). *Mind and nature: A necessary unity*. Toronto: Bantam.

Bawden, R. (2010). Messy issues, worldviews and systemic competencies. In C. P. Blackmore (Ed.), *Social learning systems and communities of practice* (pp. 89–101). London: Springer.

Bawden, R., & Reichenbach, M. (2010). Learning by experiencing: Systemics, futures thinking and scenarios. In O. Ukaga, C. Maser, & M. Reichenbach (Eds.), *Sustainable development: Principles, frameworks and case tudies* (pp. 95–115). Boca Raton, FL: CRC Press.

Bell, S., & Morse, S. (1999). *Sustainability indicators: Measuring the immeasurable?* London: Earthscan Publications.

Berger, J. (2009). *Why look at animals?* London: Penguin.

Berman, M. (1981). *The reenchantment of the world*. Ithaca: Cornell University Press.

Berman, M. (1982). *All that is solid melts into air: The experience of modernity*. New York, NY: Simon and Schuster.

Brunner, W., & Urenje, S. (2012). *The parts the whole a holistic approach to environmental and sustainability education*. Tartu: Ecoprint.

Capra, F. (1997). *The web of life: A new synthesis of mind and matter*. London: Flamingo.

Capra, F. (2003). *The hidden connections*. London: Flamingo.

Chawla, L. (1998). Significant life experiences revisited: A review of research on sources of environmental sensitivity. *The Journal of Environmental Education, 29*, 11–21.
Chen, K. H. (2010). *Asia as method.* Durham: Duke University.
Communist Party of China (2007). *Constitution of the communist party of china: Amended and adapted by 17th CPC national congress.* General program. Beijing: Governmental Printing Office.
Delorme, R. (2010). *Deep complexity and the social sciences: Experience, modelling and operationality.* Northampton: Edward Elgar.
Dryzek, J. S. (2005). *The politics of the earth* (2nd ed.). Oxford: Oxford University.
Feodorov, N. (1906). *Philosophy of the common good.* St. Petersburg: Verny.
Hall, S. (1992). The west and the rest: Discourse and power. In S. Hall & B. Gieben (Eds.), *Formations of modernity* (pp. 275–332). Cambridge: Polity Press in association with the Open University.
He, H. H. (2000). On ecological ethics in Confucian school. *Journal of Renmin University of China, 2*, 32–39.
Held, D. (1992). The development of the modern state. In S. Hall & B. Gieben (Eds.), *Formations of modernity* (pp. 71–125). Cambridge: Polity Press in association with the Open University.
Hines, J., Hungerford, H., & Tomera, A. (1986). Analysis and synthesis of research on responsible environmental behavior: A meta-analysis. *The Journal of Environmental Education, 18*(2), 1–8.
Hon, W. S. (2011). Confucianism, Korean Confucianism, and ecological discourse. *Acta Koreana, 14*, 15–40.
Kollmuss, A., & Agyeman, J. (2002). Mind the gap: Why do people act environmentally and what are the barriers to pro-environmental behavior? *Environmental Education Research, 8*, 239–260.
Melamed, Y. Y. (2012). "Omnis determinatio est negatio" – Determination, negation and self-negation in Spinoza, Kant, and Hegel. In E. Forster & Y. Y. Melamed (Eds.), *Spinoza and German idealism* (pp. 175–196). Cambridge: Cambridge University Press.
Mochalov, I. I. (1988). *Vladimir Ivanovich Vernadsky; cosmos, earth, life, man, reason-from Biosphere to Noösphere.* Retrieved from http://www.eolss.net/sample-chapters/c12/e1-01-08-08.pdf
Moran, F. (n.d.). *Buffon project. Buffon's extraordinary chapter on the beaver.* (W. Smellie, Trans. in 1781). Retrieved from http://bobarnebeck.com/Buffon.html
NAS. (2015). *Sustainability: Higher education's new fundamentalism.* New York, NY: National Association of Scholars.
Norgaard, R. B. (1994). *Development betrayed: The end of progress and a co-evolutionary revisioning of the future.* London: Routledge.
Page, S. E. (2011). *Diversity and complexity.* Princeton, NJ: Princeton University Press.
Park, J. (2011). Metamorphosis of Confucian heritage culture and the possibility of an Asian education research methodology. *Comparative Education, 47*, 381–393.
Park, J. (2016). Asian education and Asia as method. In C. M. Lam & J. Park (Eds.), *Sociological and philosophical perspectives on education in the Asia-Pacific region* pp. 205–225. Singapore: Springer.
Ro, Y. C. (1989). *Korean neo-Confucianism of Yi Yulgok.* Albany: The State University of New York.
Ro, Y. C. (2011). Ecology and cosmology: A Korean neo-Confucian approach. *Acta Koreana, 14*, 113–123.
Roerich, N. (1923/2009). *Living ethics.* Novosibirsk: Siberian Roerich Society.
Savelyeva, T. (2012). Escaping the 'structural trap' of sustainability in academia through global learning environment. In K. Bartels & K. Parker (Eds.), *Teaching sustainability* (pp. 231–241). Sterling, VA: Routledge.

Savelyeva, T. (2013). It's everybody's business: Addressing the challenge of team-teaching, partnership in global seminar. In L. Johnston (Ed.), *Higher education for sustainability: Cases, challenges, and opportunities from across the curriculum* (pp. 139–153). New York, NY: Routledge.

Savelyeva, T., & Park, J. (2012). Ecologism and complexity of campus sustainability discourse. In W. Leal (Ed.), *Environmental education, communication, and sustainability, sustainable development at universities: New horizons* (pp. 183–192). Frankfurt: Peter Lang.

Shi, G. M. (2007). *Confucian environmental ethics: The position of ethics and problems.* Retrieved from www.hfu.edu.tw/~hfuacc/pro_ethics/pdf/95-11.pdf

Solovyev, V. (1877/1988). Philosophical beginnings of whole knowledge. In V. Solovyev (Ed.), *Complete works Volume II* (pp. 140–288). Moscow: Mysl.

Spinoza, B. D. (1632-1677/1995). The letters (Spinoza 1632-1677 Netherlands Correspondence; introduction and notes by S. Barbone, L. Rice and J. Adler) (S. Shirley, Trans.). Indianapolis, Ind.: Hacket.

Sterling, S. (2001). *Sustainable education: Re-visioning learning and change.* Totnes: Green Books for the Schumacher Society.

Sterling, S. (2003). *Whole system thinking as a basis for paradigm change in education. Explorations in the context of sustainability*. Bath: University of Bath.

Subetto, A. I. (2006). *Noöspherism: Movement, ideology or new scientific and worldview system?* St. Petersburg: Noöspheric Assembly of Spiritual Ecology.

Teilhard de Chardin, P. (1955/1959). *The phenomenon of man.* New York, NY: Harper.

Thomashow, M. (2002). *Bringing the biosphere home: Learning to perceive global environmental change.* Cambridge, MA: MIT Press.

Tilbury, D., & Cooke, K. (2005). *A national review of environmental education and its contribution to sustainability in Australia: Frameworks for sustainability.* Canberra: Australian Government Department of the Environment and Heritage and the Australian Research Institute in Education for Sustainability (ARIES).

Tu, W. M. (2001). The ecological turn in new Confucian humanism: Implications for China and the World. *Dædalus: Journal of the American Academy of Arts and Sciences, 130*, 243–264.

UNESCO-UNEP. (1978). *The Tbilisi Declaration: Final report intergovernmental conference on environmental education* (UNESCO ED/MD/49). Paris: Organized by UNESCO and UNEP, Tbilisi, USSR, 14–26 October 1977.

Usoltsev, V. A. (2010). *Russian cosmism and modernity* (3rd ed.). Yekarerinburg: Ministry of Education and Science of Russian Federation.

Vernadsky, V. I. (1945). Biosphere and Noösphere. *American Scientist, 33*, 1–12.

Vernadsky, V. I. (1926/1998). *The biosphere.* New York, NY: Copernicus.

Vernadsky, V. I. (1938/2012). *The transition from the biosphere to the noösphere: Excerpts from scientific thought as a planetary phenomenon.* Washington, DC: 21st Century

Yulgok, Y. (1814/1968). *The Complete works of Yulgok* 유 서*(栗谷全書)* (O. Kwon, T. Kwon, Y. Kim, I. Kim, M. Nam, N. Sung, B. An, D. Lee, S. Lee, J. Lee, J. Lee, & S. Ha, Trans.). Seoul: Institute for the Translation of Korean Classics 고 . Retrieved from http://db.itkc.or.kr/index.jsp?bizName=MM&url=/itkcdb/text/bookListIframe.jsp?bizName=MM&seojiId=kc_mm_a201&gunchaId=&NodeId=&setid=21571 (Chinese) http://db.itkc.or.kr/index.jsp?bizName=MK&url=/itkcdb/text/bookListIframe.jsp?bizName=MK&seojiId=kc_mk_h037&gunchaId=&NodeId=&setid=21560 (Korean).

Zheng, D. F. (2010). Study of the Confucian ecologism by overseas scholars. *Journal of Poyang Lake, 105*, 34–51.

Rethinking the Concept of Sustainability: Hiroshima as a subject of peace education

KANAKO IDE

Abstract

The article discusses a sustainable educational approach for developing a moral value of peace by using a historical event, the bombing of Hiroshima. To make the case, the article uses the care theory of Nel Noddings to discuss the interpersonal aspects of peace education. The article asks how care theory handles tragedies like Hiroshima and it can contribute to a moral value of peace. The idea of caring is also examined, through Hiroshima, from a different angle, of the relationship between nature and human beings. The political position of this article is to expand the idea of sustainability by creating values for peace using material related to the bombing.

Introduction

This article is a contribution to an educational discussion for continuously cultivating the moral value of peace through the idea of interconnection. The sense of continuity and the idea of interconnection are important factors of the moral value of peace because the idea of realization of peace includes both a time axis and existences of others. The argument is developed in relation to a specific historical subject: the atomic bombing of Hiroshima in 1945. The article distinguishes educational approaches for promoting the moral value of peace from anti-war and anti-nuclear war education. This distinction is important. Since Hiroshima is a war site in world history, it has been understood as educational material for anti-war and anti-nuclear education, which teaches the importance of peace paradoxically by emphasizing the horror of war. On the contrary, this article explores alternative to anti-war and anti-nuclear rhetoric in the context of Hiroshima. Thus, the object of the article is to examine educational approaches for the value of peace as a consistent way but still applying the war event of Hiroshima as educational material.

This object is examined through the testimonies left by children who experienced the bombing. There are two reasons to apply the qualitative data. First, children's testimonies are educational materials which promote the moral value of peace consistently. Arata Osada, a Pestalozzian, a Japanese educational philosopher, and a survivor of the atomic bomb in Hiroshima, edited a book called *Genbaku No Ko*[1] (1951), a collection of experiences of the atomic bomb in Hiroshima given by 105 children, ranging in age from elementary school to college students. In preface, Osada points out that this book is material to learn peace because the texts can teach not only the misery of an atomic bomb but also the beauty of human beings. Osada argues that the bombing of Hiroshima can be the beginning of world peace because, although the atomic bomb reflects the negative nature of human beings, the children's testimonies show the affirmative side of human nature. According to Osada, this positive aspect is visible in the chaotic aftermath of the bomb, with many children describing people helping each other despite hellish circumstances. These testimonies are also pertinent because children meet the image of hope and sustainability for peace. Maria Montessori asserts that children are the teachers of peace (1949/1972). According to Montessori, children can teach adults the value of peace because they are so innocent. Osada takes a similar assumption. For example, he collected children's experiences rather than writing his own personal experience of Hiroshima, even though he was an internationally well-known scholar in education. Additionally, Osada effectively applies the image of children in promoting the image of peace and sustainability in the book. The cover of the first edition of the book is a picture of child survivors lively smiling in Hiroshima city after the war, together with photos of animated children in postwar Hiroshima. These photos do not promote the image of tragedy, but rather, indicate Osada's intention to demonstrate that life is stronger than the power of the bomb. These images also carry a sense of sustainability with regard to peace because children are a symbol of the next generation and the future.

On the other hand, even though both Montessori and Osada agree on the notion of children as teachers of peace, they would be too naïve on the current social situation. For example, it is doubtful that these children have remained ideologically innocent, because the bombing of Hiroshima has been widely debated: even 70 years later, the political debate regarding the legitimacy of the bombing still remains as strong as ever. It indicates that, in order to theorize children's experiences associated with the bombing of Hiroshima from the viewpoint of emphasizing the hope of human dignity, theoretical frameworks should be strong enough to differentiate between anti-war/nuclear issues and peace issues. For this reason, this article applies the care theory of Nel Noddings, an American feminist philosopher, to its interpretation of these children's experiences. Noddings' theoretical framework is appropriate in distancing this article from the debate over justice in Hiroshima, because her initial standpoint establishes a theoretical distance from the binary of just and unjust (1984). At the same time, Noddings' care theory allows us to interpret the children's Hiroshima testimonies with a sense of continuity, because the aim of her theory is to value interpersonal aspects. For these reasons, this article reinterprets the children's testimonies in the context of care theory. The article also conducts a critical examination of care theory by reflecting on qualitative data. For instance, some children described their relationship with nature in their testimonies. To understand the significant aspects of this relationship that are not illuminated by care theory, the testimonies will be analyzed with the concept of 'dependent origination' found in Buddhist philosophy.

Peace and caring

Noddings' care theory characterizes the idea of caring as feminine because the bond between 'mother' and 'caring' is considered the tightest of all. In addition, the starting point of caring and being cared for is sharing emotions rather than appealing to reason. Noddings also believes that caring is intrinsic to human nature because mothers naturally care for their children. According to Noddings (1984), 'we find ourselves at the center of concentric circles of caring' (p. 46). For her, each individual has an enclosure in which his or her caring is influential. Then, within these boundaries, there are limited others having strong ties with that person. However, this does not mean that there is no way of approaching caring outside of the enclosure, because it is possible to extend the circles of care throughout one's life. For instance, although originally there is no direct connection between mothers and sons-in-law, they become caring to each other through her child or his partner. Noddings calls this growth the 'chain of caring'. This relationship of cared and cared for is characterized as the receptivity of caring. It is neither dependency nor self-sacrificial altruism. In the context of social ethics, there is a relationship between the action maker who cares and the action receiver who is cared for.

Since Noddings' idea of caring is divided into three gradations: caring, the chain of caring, and caring about, this article proposes to frame the children's testimonies in these same three graduations. I wish to note here that the educational approach of this research does not seek to demonstrate a practical teaching method in a classroom setting, but to theoretically interpret a way of learning peace by reading testimonies as a sort of continuous educational activity of the hermeneutic circle. Therefore, in this context, the educational approach involves reading the testimonies three times. Within this learning method, the 'teacher' denotes the texts written by the children of Hiroshima, and 'learners' denotes readers of the text. Some might be concerned that care theory discusses an education of actual human relationships, not of reading books. However, care theory says that reading books is an effective educational experience for developing empathy. Also, in the context of the event of the atomic bombing of Hiroshima, this approach should be defended as a way of learning because these children's testimonies were originally written and preserved with the aim of making history. Seventy years on, the survivors' population has decreased. Learners are soon going to lose all opportunity to have face-to-face relationships with survivors. For this reason, the reading of historical testimony is identifiable as an educational opportunity about care.

To initiate Noddings' gradations of caring, readers firstly need to establish a circle of caring toward the children who relayed their experiences. This means taking the book in hand, opening, and starting to read. The reading attitude, however, should be educationally considered. Henry David Thoreau (1946) discusses the importance of the quality of reading. In *Walden*, he says, 'Books must be read as deliberately and reservedly as they were written …' because

> … to read well, that is, to read true books in a true spirit, is a noble exercise, and one that will task the reader more than any exercise which the customs of the day esteem. It requires a training such as the athletes underwent, the steady intention almost of the whole life to this object. (p. 117)

In Osada's evaluation, because the testimonies were written by children, they have some technical and grammatical immaturity. However, Osada notices that these problems cannot be a cause for underestimating the quality of testimony. According to Osada, the children's writings are powerful enough to touch audiences and to develop their empathy. Audiences are able to establish the circle of care with the children in the book by naturally sharing their feelings through developing sincere reading attitudes.

The chain of caring begins in reading the texts with self-reflection, and in thinking on the influence of care. All the survivors express their struggles to survive, despite their despair. In addition to the deep sorrows caused by the loss of their own family members, survivors had to live with the horror of others' deaths. One child writes, 'The person who cheerfully talked to me yesterday was as dead as mutton this morning. I was very scared that it might happen to me next' (Osada, 1951, p. 230). According to another testimony, 'Everywhere the dead and wounded were lying about covered with dirt and blood. The wounded were groaning and each had someone on his mind he was calling to' (Osada, 1951, p. 123). Another survivor says, 'A woman who was apparently a mother, her body all covered with blood, went running by calling a child's name' (Osada, 1951, p. 158). Audiences can find that many survivors experienced and witnessed these scenes of care. These testimonies could lead audiences to think about their interpretations and understanding of historical facts. Under these conditions, what does caring mean for survivors? Some survivors wrote about caring for other victims. Some children witnessed that what victims wanted at the point of death was to be cared for by those who were deeply in their circle of care. Others testify that a mother who was badly injured was still caring for her child, more than for herself. These testimonies promote audiences to deliberate the various kinds of caring that were happening in Hiroshima right after the bomb.

The next gradation is to read texts from the viewpoint of 'caring about'. Here is one child's experience: 'A survivor found the charred bodies of students and a teacher. The dead bodies were placed in such a way as to indicate that the teacher had tried to protect the students at the last moment' (Osada, 1951, p. 95). Osada interprets this episode as proof that human beings are not fundamentally selfish, but rather that they are respectable creatures, because people try to help others even in hellish circumstances. This analysis has a synthesis with Noddings' argument. Since students were inside the teacher's circle of care, the teacher tried to protect them. In addition, some victims cared for those who were outside of their care circle. Here is a testimony written by a survivor who was a 3rd-grade student at the time:

> In front of Mother a girl was sitting who was just about my age. Her whole body was covered with burns and wounds and she was bleeding. She seemed to be in great pain and she kept calling her mother; but all of a sudden she asked my mother, 'Please, lady, is your child here?'
>
> That was because the child couldn't see any longer.
>
> Mother answered her, 'Yes, she is.'

> Then the girl said, 'Please give this to your child,' and she held out something.
>
> It was her lunch box. This was the lunch that her mother had fixed for her and given to her that morning when she left for school.
>
> 'Don't you want to eat it yourself?' Mother asked. 'I am going to die. Give it to your daughter.'
>
> We accepted it. For a while we went down the river and as the boat reached the sea that child said, 'Lady, I'll tell you my name and if you should meet my mother tell her that I am here, will you?' and as she said it she drew her last breath and died.
>
> I was terribly, terribly sorry for her. Mother and I wept together. I cannot imagine how happy I would be now, if that child were alive. (Osada, 1951, p. 113)

According to the testimony, the writer and her mother did not know the victim until they accidentally found themselves together in the same boat for evacuation. The victim was severely injured and desperately asking to be cared for by her mother. Compared to the victim, the writer of this testimony was fortunate because she was under the care of her own mother in the situation. Interestingly, however, the circle of care as well as the chain of care was promoted by the person who, of all three, needed to be cared for the most. The victim had no hope of receiving what she wanted at the verge of death—to be with her mother and to receive her mother's care. Nevertheless, as the testimony shows, she cared for those whom she did not know through the gift of her lunch box, the symbol of her mother's care before school that morning. The girl knew that she was giving her lunch box to the person who had all that she wanted—to be with her own mother, and not to be in pain. Additionally, the testimony shows how the establishment of this caring relationship in the boat continued long after the girl passed away, because the writer testifies that she still cares for the injured girl. Here, the reading testimony turns out a powerful lesson of caring and human dignity. How can victims and survivors establish and even maintain a sense of caring under such horrible circumstances? These testimonies teach audiences that caring is part of human nature; people *just do* act like this, especially in such environments. The tragic events have the capacity to bring out our unconditional love, and to break the conventions of care that usually only extend to those who are already close to us. Although people were in despair, they were still able to care for each other.

Flower power and the idea of dependent origination

As described above, Noddings' theory provides a useful way of reframing the testimonies collected by Osada from the aspect of caring. The beauty of human nature visible in the testimonies offers audiences hope for peace by teaching human dignity in the process of hermeneutical education. On the other hand, reading children's testimonies from the viewpoint of connection invites audiences to go beyond care theory, because these data are rich enough to further examination of the moral value of peace. In addition to the caring among victims, many survivors also discussed nature in their testimony. For instance, a survivor looked back on her experience as follows,

> A doctor said to us that 'since your mother is dying, give her whatever she wants to eat'. My brother and me yelled at the doctor, 'Charlatan!' and cried in the backyard. At that time, I felt that only shining stars in the sky understood our sorrow and cared for us. (Osada, 1951, p. 279)

This survivor wrote that she felt she received 'care' from nature, even though humans had given up caring for her and her family. There is another story associated with nature, relationship, and Hiroshima. Oleander, called *Kyouchikutou* in Japanese, became the flower of the Hiroshima city for the following reason. After the bombing, some scientists estimated that there would be barren land for 75 years because of severe pollution. In fact, there was a plan to rebuild Hiroshima in some other place and abandon the old Hiroshima City. Yet, the *Kyouchikutou* flower gave hope to the people that the city could be reconstructed, by emerging from the polluted ground.[2] People gained encouragement from this natural, non-human phenomenon. The blooming flowers encouraged them to have hope, providing an example of life emerging from death and desolation, and showing them the victory of life over incalculable odds. Another survivor wrote that 'spring is also coming again even in Hiroshima. People were very impressed when a weed came to bud on the area estimated to be burnt-out for 75 years' (Osada, 1951, p. 253). People seemed to be deeply impressed by the aspects of nature that they might otherwise ignore in ordinary circumstances.

There are two ways to interpret these experiences using Noddings' argument. One is that these are just misinterpretations by survivors. According to Noddings, caring is limited to human beings that have the ability to be involved in the circle of caring. Noddings believes that, although human life is supported by the activity of plants, this is not caring. Only human beings can care. The plants could stand only as a symbol that allows us to imagine survivor linking to survivor through shared witnessing of the seeming impossibility of life emerging from barrenness. In other words, nature promotes the expansion of the chain of caring, but only as a symbol.

However, Noddings' interpretation of nature and care is less persuasive. Oleander became the flower of Hiroshima city because many survivors felt that by their blooming, the Oleanders themselves encouraged the people in Hiroshima after the bombing. Through the Oleanders, those in distress were able to feel that they were being cared for by nature—a contrast to Noddings' claims that only people can care for each other. This distinction stands apart from the assumption that Noddings' model stands on individualism. There seems to be a limit to what caring, as a human-to-human model of relationships, can do here. The notion of caring, though correct, seems perhaps to be too humanistic and too individualistic to work as a full interpretation of the children's testimonies. For instance, Noddings discusses each individual as the 'center' of their own caring, and the circle of caring as expanding from the center outward. She does not mean that each individual is isolated, but rather that the self-identification lies is the connection between oneself and others, because humans are social animals. However, 'others' mean only humans—not plants or animals. On the contrary, survivors' testimonies in Hiroshima include nature as one of 'us' as survivors.

Therefore, in order to understand the testimony's associations with nature from the viewpoint of relationship, it is necessary to apply another theoretical framework for the third reading. Here are the conditions of the alternative theoretical framework. This alternative theory should take the same basic assumption of interconnection that care theory does. At the same time, it should be theoretically more inclusive than Noddings' care theory, in order to incorporate the discussion about nature.

This article therefore applies the Buddhist philosophical idea of *dependent origination* (縁起), which is a part of social foundation in Buddhist-oriented societies like Japan. The notion of 'dependent origination' is a form of connection, in which

> ... all beings and phenomena exist or occur in relation to other beings or phenomena. All things are linked in an intricate web of causation and connection, and nothing, whether in the realm of human affairs or natural phenomena, can exist or occur solely of its own accord. Greater emphasis is placed on the interdependent relationships between individuals than on the individual alone. (Ikeda, 1996, p. 210)

The idea of dependent origination understands that all creatures are originally interconnected. It should be noted here that, due to different stands of social foundations, 'dependency' in this context includes the idea of interdependency, though this sense is not well captured by its English equivalent. 'Dependency' does make sense in the context of Buddhist-oriented society because it fits with its social norm of 'modesty'. Thus, dependency does not signify an immature or unfair relationship in this context. Rather, it emphasizes the necessity of others. The idea of dependency origination as a social foundation turns into religious faith when it is believed in accordance with *Dharma* (Sanskrit) (Pali dhamma)—a sort of natural law[3]—explaining the connection of creatures and phenomena ultimately. For example, *The Lotus Sutra*[4] explains the connection between human beings, other creatures, the cosmos, and even previous life and death. Ethics cannot be discussed only as a human issue in Buddhism's idea of dependency because it assumes that each life is already linked, without any discrimination.

The sense of interdependency as dependent origination has two characters. First, it is a way of understanding phenomena. The concept of phenomena, when understood as a reflection of interconnection, is what Buddhism calls causation.

> To speak of discovering the true entity 'behind' phenomena might give the impression that the Law exists somewhere apart from the phenomena. This is definitely not the case. Phenomena and their true entity are always inseparable. The Buddha observes the true entity as it manifests through phenomena and correctly perceives that the true entity exists only as the phenomena. They certainly do not exist separately. (Ikeda, 1997, p. 139)

Causation in Buddhism weaves into the fabric of the phenomenal world. In fact, it is proper to consider causation in Buddhism as more organic and relational: Buddhist causation is not limited to causation in the scientific or physicists' sense. Causation is also both intrinsic and extrinsic: causation not only takes place through the influence or relation of one being upon another, but through a being's own capacity to self-influence or self-relate. 'Your life thus becomes a cause ("internal cause") and, activated by your conditions internal and external ("relation"), changes arise in your life ("latent effect"), and these eventually appear externally ("manifest effect")' (Ikeda, 1997, p. 136). This is how dependent origination sees the connection not only of human phenomena but also any phenomena in nature. The second aspect of *dependent origination* in Buddhism is that it is a way of understanding subjectivity. As I described above, the foundational idea of dependency not only emphasizes interrelationships, but also believes in the transformation of each individual. Since each individual's life is connected to the universe, each person's changes are microscopic, and synchronous with the cosmos. In this context, caring is an interaction between the giver and the receiver. At the same time, the action of caring eventually is for the care herself/himself, who cares.

As the theoretical framework of reading texts as an educational activity is transformed from the concept of care to the concept of *dependent origination*, so it is retranslated as a way of understanding the process of educational experience. Within the framework of Thoreau's idea about the importance of the quality of reading, Stanley Cavell proposes the quantity of reading in *The Senses of Walden*. He says, 'On the first perusal plain common sense should appear—on the second serve truth—and on a third serve beauty' (p. 1). As already described in the context of care theory, audiences firstly need to learn the attitude with which to read the book which then becomes an establishment of the care circle. Then, through the first reading, the audiences learn the fact of Hiroshima to develop the gradation of caring. Through the second reading, the audiences cultivate the gradation of caring by capturing the truth of human nature from the texts. As for the third reading, the audiences start reading the texts with the aspect of *dependent origination*. According to Cavell, the third reading experience becomes an esthetic educational experience for readers. This will also allow readers to develop limitlessly their imagination with regard to the dignity of human life—not just in terms of human society, but in terms of all lives, including the natural world. The third reading experience gives freedom for readers to explore the testimony because the idea of interconnection reflected on phenomena is presumed to be something beyond the understanding of human beings. Audiences are allowed to freely imagine the mysterious experience of a survivor who felt that stars in the sky gave her more comfort than the doctor who was actually treating her mother at the phenomenal level. In the tale of the Oleander, how are survivors spiritually influenced by the blooming of flowers? What did it mean for survivors to sense the coming of spring after being bombed? Moreover, the phenomenon of human relationship can go deeper with creating another hermeneutic circle. For example, the story of the lunch box asks: is this accidentally happened?, or did they met by accident? Reading testimonies now becomes an opportunity to deliberate human nature and the interconnectness of lives.

Conclusion

The article explored an educational discussion to foster the moral value of peace through the example of Hiroshima. It focused on Nel Noddings' model of caring, critically examining her idea of caring by using it to evaluate the educational value of young survivors' testimonies, and through doing so, concluded that it is necessary to allow a social and educational role for both nature and the supranatural notion of dependent origination. The article applied the basic idea of Buddhist philosophy, dependency, to the idea of caring in order to increase the capacity of the discussion on peace. In addition to expanding the parameters of caring, the idea of dependent origination presented deeper questions about the relationship between human nature and caring.[5]

Disclosure statement

No potential conflict of interest was reported by the author.

Notes

1. The book has been translated into over 17 languages.
2. See Hiroshima City (xxx).
3. Note that the closest Western equivalent to this line of thinking is German idealism: the idea of Geist, or mindfulness, in which everything stands in relation to everything else as an (interconnected) whole.
4. Note that the following quote from The Lotus Sutra. 'Ignorance causes action, action causes consciousness, consciousness causes name and form, name and form cause the six sense organs, the six sense organs cause contact, contact causes sensation, sensation causes desire, desire causes attachment, attachment causes existence, existence causes birth, birth causes old age and death, worry and grief, suffering and anguish. If ignorance is wiped out, then action will be wiped out. If action is wiped out, then consciousness will be wiped out. If consciousness is wiped out, then name and form will be wiped out. If name and form are wiped out, then the six sense organs will be wiped out. If contact is wiped out, then sensation will be wiped out. If desire is wiped out, then attachment will be wiped out. If attachment is wiped out, then existence will be wiped out. If existence is wiped out, then birth will be wiped out. If birth is wiped out, then old and death, worry and grief, suffering and anguish will be wiped out' (The Lotus Sutra, 1993, p. 131).
5. The author thanks Dr Cris Mayo for her generous support.

References

Cavell, S. (1992). *The senses of Walden: An expanded edition*. London: The University of Chicago Press.

Hiroshima City. (xxx). *City Three and City Flower*. Retrieved from http://www.city.hiroshima•α.lg.jp/www/contents/1112000428867/index.html

Ikeda, D. (1996). *A new humanism: The university addresses of Daisaku Ikeda.* New York, NY: Weatherhill.

Ikeda, D. (1997). *Lecture on the 'Expedient Means' and 'Life Span' chapters of the Lotus Sutra.* New York, NY: World Tribune Press.

Montessori, M. (1949/1972). *Education and peace.* (H. R. Lane, Trans.). Thiruvanmiyur: Kalakshetra Press.

Noddings, N. (1984). *Caring, a feminine approach to ethics and moral education.* Berkeley: University of California Press.

Osada, A. (1951). *Genbaku No Ko* [Children of the A-bomb: Testament of the boys and girls of Hiroshima]. Tokyo: Iwanami Shoten.

Osada, A. (1963). *Children of the A-bomb: Testament of the boys and girls of Hiroshima.* (J. Dan, & R. Sieben-Morgen, Trans). New York, NY: Putnam.

The Lotus Sutra. (1993). (B. Watson, Trans.). New York, NY: Columbia University Press.

Thoreau, H. D. (1946). *Walden.* New York, NY: The Vail-Ballou Press.

Educating the Heart and the Mind: Conceptualizing inclusive pedagogy for sustainable development

MOUSUMI MUKHERJEE

Abstract

There is growing global consensus that inequality is making sustainable development goals unattainable. Social inclusion of the historically marginalized and equality of opportunity is crucial for sustainable development. Inclusive quality education for all is therefore considered as one of the three main targets for sustainable development according to UNESCO's Incheon declaration in 2015. This paper draws on an institutional ethnography of a globally interconnected old colonial school's inclusive pedagogic work in postcolonial India. The school's work has been much celebrated in existing research by academics, global donor agencies and also by the Indian government's Sarva Shikshya Abhiyan (Education for All) office. This paper analyses how the school conceptualized a distinct inclusive pedagogy to educate the hearts and the minds of children driven by local community needs for social inclusion within a context of extreme inequality. This paper argues that the school's conception of inclusive education addressing the diverse learning needs of children developed as a syncretic cultural formation drawing on its institutional mission for social justice, as well as indigenous history of educational reform and philosophy of community engagement. In doing so, this paper engages with the 'philosophy of context' and draws on the 'southern theory' of inclusive education as envisioned by Rabindranath Tagore, indigenous education reformer and Nobel Laureate poet activist during early twentieth-century colonial British India, who challenged both local and global inequality through his creative and educational work.

Introduction

The case study school for this research is now part of a large global network of Catholic schools for girls operating in 24 countries and 6 continents. This paper argues how the inclusive pedagogic reforms instituted by the school were a syncretic cultural formation which followed the unique institutional history of the particular Catholic order in India, as well cultural history of educational reform and progressive 'philosophy of context' (Peters, 2012) in the region where the school is located in India. This analytic and hermeneutic engagement is guided by evidence gathered through ethnographic research. The inclusive reforms have been already studied through Deweyian and Freirean analytical lens by other scholars who have studied the work of this school (Bajaj, 2011a, 2011b; Greene, 1995). This paper analyses the genealogy of these reforms in establishing inclusive pedagogy bridging social inequality for holistic education of every child through the critical 'southern theoretical' (Connell, 2007) lens of Rabindranath Tagore, as it is evident from his educational writings and experiments in his school in Shantiniketan,[1] which emphasized not just social inclusion and inclusive learning for all, but also youth social action—a model of education which combined the heart and the mind of children for community engagement and development. In the next section of this essay, I will first describe the context and the case study before engaging in theoretical discussion about Tagore's Southern Theory of inclusive education and how it is useful to analyse and interpret the school's inclusive educational work within a context of deep inequality.

The Hybridized Context

The context of Delphine Hart School[2] is a hybridized postcolonial context where historically 'congeries of global and local interactions' (Vavrus & Bartlett, 2006) shaped the history of the community, the social imaginary of the people and global network of connections for the school. The postcolonial city of Kolkata, where the school is located, was the colonial capital of British India, Calcutta. The city witnessed turbulent and violent geopolitical history of the region with hungry people pouring out of the rural villages to die on the streets of the city during the Bengal famine of World War II[3]. Thereafter, the city witnessed bloody communal violence during the partition of South Asia to form two nations—India and Pakistan in 1947, and later Bangladesh formed out of East Pakistan in the early 1970s.

These histories of conflict, violence and struggles did not just span for about 40 years since the early 1940s to the 1970s; it was preceded by freedom struggle against colonial rule for almost a century.[4] This long history of conflict had depleted the economic resources of the region badly. Moreover, colonial policies had further enhanced the ideological and social divides among the indigenous elite population as argued by Mukherjee-Reed (2008) citing Indian historian Sumit Sarkar (1983) and Islamic liberation theologian, reformer and social activist, Ashgar Ali Engineer's (1985) work among other sources. Mukherjee-Reed (2008, p. 60) further argues: 'The [partition] movement, in this sense, was a clear response of the elite to the threats to the bases of their social power emerging from colonialism (Alavi 2002).' As a consequence of this historic divide, the rising tide of refugees from East Pakistan and later Bangladesh in the postcolonial era compounded the social problems of poverty and homelessness in the region. According to one estimate as cited by Kumar (2009), 250,000 Hindus and as many Muslims migrated to India every year from Bangladesh (earlier East Pakistan) since 1951.

Delphine Hart School

Against the backdrop of this turbulent context, Delphine Hart School was established by the Jesuitess[5] missionary order in 1857. Education within the Indian context has been historically very privatized and more so for the girl's education sector, since:

> the education of women was not high on the agenda in Britain at that time, and the small resources to be devoted to educating England's Indian subjects were not be wasted on the lower classes or on women. Thus the earliest efforts at providing formal education for girls came from private agency- from the private initiative of colonial officials and most notably from missionaries (Seth, 2007, p. 137)

Though colonialism and missionary work are often conflated, not just within the popular social imaginary but also by comparative education scholars, such as Carnoy (1974); some historians of Indian education have argued with evidence about the wide diversity of missionary activities within colonial South Asia (Bara, 2000; Bellenoit, 2014). They argue that often missionary work was at loggerheads with colonial agenda.

Noted Indian critical theorist, Spivak (1994), who studied in a missionary school in immediate postcolonial times in Calcutta as a child, has also testified that:

> By the time I was going [to school], most of the teachers were tribal Christians, this is to say, Indian subalterns, lower than rural underclass by origin, neither Hindus nor Muslims, not even Hindu untouchables, but tribals- so called aboriginals- who had been converted by missionaries (p. 274).

This is a great testimony from a noted scholar about the subversive work of some of the Christian missionaries among subaltern indigenous communities within the colonial Indian context. It can be argued here that in many ways some of the missionary activities within the South Asian context were similar to the missionary activities in Latin America, which gave rise to Liberation Theology in the 1950s–1960s (Berryman, 1987; Brown, 1993; Clarke, 1998).

The case study school also bears the legacy of a unique transnational history with regard to its origin. A German Priest, who served as an apostolic in the Bengal province of British India and later settled in Australia, took initiative to bring the Jesuitess nuns from Ireland to setup schools in the Bengal region for minority poor Catholic girls there. They were mostly daughters of poor Irish and English soldiers, and some mixed-race descendants of Portuguese, French and other Europeans with Indians (known as Eurasians[6] during colonial times). Due to great deal of sectarianism among the European Christian communities, the Anglican colonial British government was apparently indifferent about the education of this population. (Nolan, 2008) Therefore, though the schools were set up to serve a marginalized population within the colonial context, nonetheless, they were racially exclusive because they served a specific Catholic (mostly European) community within the colonial Indian context.

However, through the course of its long history, the schools run by the order of Jesuitess went through waves of changes in their admissions policy to become progressively more inclusive of Indian children from all backgrounds. From being racially segregated, the schools became progressively racially inclusive of Indian children. Interestingly, though the schools were originally envisioned to serve the poor Catholic girls in the region by the German Priest, over the passage of time, the schools became exclusive in terms of social class stratification of the student body. This was because of 'injustice in the educational policy' as affirmed by the Jesuitess school historian, Colmcille (1968), since schools would be provided generous funds by the colonial government only if 'they catered for a class whose standard of living was considerably higher than that of the average Indian family' (p. 280). Therefore, separate free schools for the poor Indian girls would be operated to meet the social justice mission of the institution. This has been well documented by Colmcille (1968) in her historical account of the school's work.

Changing Dynamics for Social Inclusion

In the immediate postcolonial era, the free schools were closed and Jesuitess schools kept a small percentage (about 20%) of their seats reserved for poor Catholic girls, corresponding to their Catholic mission for social justice and were mostly engaged in educating the daughters of native middleclass and social elites from Hindu, Muslim and Anglo-Indian families. However, following the turbulent postcolonial context of the 1970s, Delphine Hart School particularly changed its admission policy since the late 1970s. Over three decades since late 1970s, the school had been serving the needs of large numbers of poor students irrespective of their religious background. According to existing literature on the school's work, 50% of the total student body comes from very poor socioeconomic backgrounds (Bajaj, 2011a; Chattopadhay, 2015; Doggett, 2005; Greene, 1995; Jessop, 1998). It is to be noted here that this policy along with several other policies and practices were changing over the three years period of my ethnographic fieldwork due to various constraints in recent years (Mukherjee, 2015). However, there is enough evidence to demonstrate that prior to the recent changes; the school has been strategically utilizing range of financial, intellectual and human resources through its global Jesuitess network to meet the needs of the large body of underserved disadvantaged students admitted in their school. The school was also engaging with various local community outreach programs for social equity and human rights.

In 1994, the school became a recipient of UNESCO NOMA Prize for spreading literacy in the region. The school Principal also got invited in several education conferences to deliver workshops on values education and staff transformation seminars for inclusive pedagogy nationally and internationally, contributing to national and regional policy debates on school leadership. Since the mid-1990s, a number of independent academic studies and studies by global development agencies have been studying, celebrating and citing the work of this school for addressing a range of issues regarding inclusive education and development in the region. The school's work has been studied as a model of best practices for values driven low cost-effective schooling because of its optimal use of resources in a study funded by DFID (Jessop, 1998). It has been studied through the critical lens of Deweyian 'experiential learning' for community engagement among students by Greene (1995). Its work has been studied through gender critical lens by Doggett (2005). It has been also studied through Freirean critical lens for its values-based 'critical consciousness' raising human rights education by Bajaj (2011). Most recently, Chattopadhay (2015) has studied the work of the school as a successful example of purposive social inclusion, where middleclass girls are active stakeholders for the education and welfare of the girls from subaltern backgrounds.

The school's work was also cited as one of the successful case studies in the Indian Government's Sarva Sikshya Abhiyan (Education for All) publication (MHRD, 2011). Prior to that, in 2007 the school's Principal was awarded the fourth highest civilian award by the Indian Government. The school's work was publicized as operating like a central hub for 'social transformation' coordinating the community outreach programmes like the spokes of a wheel in collaboration with donor agencies, such as the UNICEF, Institute for Human Rights Education, Save the Children, Indian Government's Sarva Sikshya Abhiyan (Education for All) Office, Union Ministry of Women and Child Welfare and several other corporate beneficiaries. The school became engaged in coordinating several community outreach projects to share resources with neighboring village schools, provide teacher's training for a range of para-teachers, as well as government school teachers, develop curriculum for human rights education and also established satellite schools for migrant children in the brickfields situated towards the outer-fringes of the city of Calcutta and among fishing communities in a neighboring Indian state.

Evidence from this research shows that, even prior to the global discourse on EFA and inclusive educational reform in the 1990s, the school has been instituting inclusive reforms driven by local community needs. The school's 'Ripples and Rainbow' booklet states:

> Started in 1979 at [Delphine Hart School], a school already in existence since 1857, this experiment was born of a certain uneasiness felt at being part of a formal school system imparting 'quality education' to a privileged few, while millions of their less fortunate peer group get virtually nothing at all.

With the rise in the global discourse on EFA for social inclusion and Human Rights Education, the school appeared to be utilizing these global discourses strategically to promote its own work nationally and globally by gathering consent from local parents, making middleclass girls and their parents active stakeholders for the education of marginalized subaltern girls[7] within the hierarchical Indian postcolonial society for inclusive development. As Reinke (2004) had argued following research on indigenous education in Mexico, the rise of the global discourse on Education for All since the 1990s was actually benefiting the inclusive work that the school had already begun about a decade ago driven by the local needs of the community.

However, within a context of deep inequality and deeply rooted social class biases reinforced by the influence of class prejudice driven Victorian England, how was this possible? Why was 'a certain uneasiness felt' by the Delphine Hart School community members, unlike most missionary/convent English-medium schools within that context imparting 'quality education to a privileged' few? There is no doubt that the inclusive pedagogic reforms were driven by local needs following the turbulent political history and changes in the political economy of the region. However, I argue here that the progressive reforms for social inclusion at the Delphine Hart School since 1979 were also a product of the institutional history of the Jesuitess order, transformational school leadership and progressive cultural history of educational reform in the region. They were happening at the intersection of institutional context, institutional beliefs and school leader's core beliefs, as Harris and Johnston (2010) argued while theorizing values-based school leadership.

The progressive changes at the school to institutionalize inclusive educational reforms were, therefore, not happening within a cultural vacuum. The intercultural experiences of key-actors within the school were crucial in conceptualizing the school's distinct philosophy of engagement to educate the hearts and the minds of children making middle class girls active-stakeholders in the education and empowerment of their less privileged peers for equality and sustainable development. Besley and Peters (2011) cite Bohm et al., (1991) stating that, 'Dialog ... enables inquiry into, and understanding of, the sorts of processes that fragment and interfere with real communication between individuals, nations and even different parts of the same organization'. (p. 5). Here, it should be noted that the historic legacy of progressive social and educational reforms in the region was also a product of the colonial history of the region and intercultural dialogue between the colonizer and the colonized over centuries. This argument will be further expanded in the following section.

Bengal Renaissance

The Bengal region of India in particular holds the legacy of several progressive social reform movements since the early nineteenth century, known as the Bengal renaissance following the global heritage of the European enlightenment. A number of educated Indian men took lead in promoting progressive social reforms in the region during this time, which included negotiating with the British governors to impose ban on 'suttee'[8] (widow burning), promote widow remarriage and education of women in particular. These men were part of the indigenous social reform movement, popularly known as the Bengal Renaissance. During this time, the Brahmo Samaj[9] and several schools for girls were established. First Indian Nobel Laureate poet and indigenous education reformer, Rabindranath Tagore's grandfather and father were also part of this movement.

This intellectual history of the region also influenced some of the Jesuitess nuns and teachers working in the school. This includes the school historian, Mother Mary Colmcille. Historic archival data gathered as part of the ethnographic case study of the school show that the school staff and leadership had been engaged in serious intercultural dialog with the native indigenous spiritual traditions outside of the Catholic order and the intellectual history of the region. They have been engaging with progressive indigenous social reform traditions by recruiting teachers trained in the Brahmo tradition of schooling. Moreover, some of the Jesuitess nuns and school staff have been particularly engaged with the literary and pedagogic work of Rabindranath Tagore. The Jesuitess school historian, Mother Mary Colmcille was particularly enamoured of Tagore's progressive social reform ideas drawing on indigenous myths and historic characters expressed through creative art. She was also a teacher of Bengali and produced several plays and dance dramas created by Tagore with strong message for social inclusion and reform during school functions.

Hence, in the following section of the paper, I will expand on Tagore's 'southern theory'[10] of inclusive education. Tagore's pedagogic reform in his experimental school during colonial India sought to address the diverse needs of learners as against the colonial 'factory-model' (Tagore, 1906) of schooling during his times. As a famous school dropout, Tagore's educational theory was based on his own experience of schooling. During a lecture tour in the US, Tagore stated openly that, 'It was not any new theory of education, but the memory of my school-days … For it has given me knowledge of the wrong from which the children of men suffer' (Tagore, 1917). Moreover, Tagore gave emphasis to holistic education of every child, which also involved intercultural education and community engagement for sustainable development. This kind of pedagogic approach has been referred to as 'education for fullness' by Mukherjee (2013).

'Southern Theory' and 'Philosophy of Context'

'Southern Theory' is a sociological term established by Raewyn Connell (2007), who argued for the inadequacy of applying theoretical formulations from Northern European countries to analyze sociological problems and data from Southern postcolonial countries. It highlights the global politics of knowledge, since the global South has been historically treated as a data mine, while the global North has been associated with the intellectual work of generating theory. In many ways, Connell's (2007) arguments move beyond Chakrabarty's (2007) arguments in 'Provincializing Europe' about the inadequacy of established theoretical formulations within Western academia to properly understand social phenomenon in complex postcolonial contexts and suggests that 'theory too must be deimperialized', as Chen (2010) argued. Connell (2007) begins with a critical examination of the hidden assumptions driving the work of several established social theorists from Euro-American background to emphasize the need to study the work of intellectuals from Southern postcolonial contexts in order to develop better understanding of the problems within these contexts. Hence, I argue here that Peters (2012) arguments about 'philosophy of context' drawing on Wittgenstein's notion of epistemic contextualism and importance of language is useful in engaging with Tagore's 'southern theory' of inclusive education. It is useful for both analytic (ideological) and hermeneutic (affective historical) engagement with ethnographic data to analyze the case study school's inclusive pedagogic work to institutionalize education for all. More so because it is evident that the school historian, as well as several teachers at the school, were philosophically influenced by Tagore's ideas and engaged with his creative work in the local language. Most significant of them is the school historian Mother Mary Colmcille (1968), as noted earlier. Therefore, in the following sections of this chapter I will engage with Tagore's writings on education and society theoretically to analyze the school's inclusive pedagogic approach to educate the hearts and minds of students.

Tagore's 'Southern Theory' of Inclusive Education

Tagore's theoretical ideas on education developed from his own experience of being a misfit in colonial 'factory-model' (Tagore, 1906) of schools and his deep observations of education systems abroad and comparative reflections on the needs of Indian society. Here are Tagore's main theoretical ideas as, I have gleaned from reading series of essays (originally in his mother tongue Bengali) written by Tagore since 1892 and reading the work of scholars who have read and analyzed Tagore's work (Bannerji, 2016; Bhattacharya, 2013; Collins, 2007; Dasgupta, 2009; Ghosh, 2015; Ghosh, Naseem, & Vijh, 2010; Guha, 2013; Jalan, 1976; Mukherjee, 2013; O'Connell, 2003, 2010; Pridmore, 2009; Saha, 2013; Samuel, 2011; Tagore, 1892, 1906, 1912, 1917, 1929, 2008):

- Education is a relational process between the child, teacher, peers and nature (environment).
- Child's Experience is central to the educational process.
- Curriculum and pedagogic approach should revolve around the child's aptitude and ability.
- Teacher's role is central to the pedagogic process in nurturing creativity and critical thinking (as against preparing kids for tests by rote-memorizing school textbooks).
- Education for the whole-child, which 'nourishes the heart and the intellect' (Tagore, 1906)—involving social and emotional learning—as well as for vocation (livelihood).
- Education should be community-oriented and should foster values of cooperation as against competition.
- Education should also foster intercultural learning to promote global consciousness to counter hatred based on cultural misunderstandings.

However, such progressive model of child-centered community-oriented pedagogy which focuses on holistic child development involving social and emotional learning is mostly neglected within the rigid curriculum and test-result oriented performative system of mainstream Indian education even today. The adverse effect of such a system is acknowledged very well by the long-serving Principal of Delphine Hart School since the late 1970s. This is evident from the following quote from an interview:

> Many of the schools are rife with competition. Competition means that the child who gets the highest marks gets the best price every year. This makes the parents also rabid. Now they want their children to get the first prize. So, the first thing I have to tackle is this children being pitted against each other for competition. Now when you get rid of that and bring in the idea of the community values, not competitive values, then you have already practically won the battle. Because if you have these competitive values

> when people are competing for half a mark, they are not going to stay back in the afternoon to help a poor child. They want to get their marks. They want tuition. But, when you remove that, then you compete with yourself. You strive for excellence at the level of your own potential, not someone else's. And, this relieves the children of a lot of pressure because they don't have to measure up to come first. They can all get the prize if they work hard enough. You will find a year after that the children will be willing to work for other children because the pressure is off them.
>
> —Sister Valentine

This competitive model of modern schooling system emerged within India during Victorian colonial times. Growing up as a sensitive child within the progressive home environment of his Brahmo family, Tagore was deeply influenced by western enlightenment ideals as well as the philosophical ideals of the ancient Indian, Upanishads[11]. However, Tagore was a complete failure within nineteenth-century colonial 'factory-model' of schools, which he later critiqued in several of his essays and his famous satirical short story- 'The Parrot's Training'[12]. In a talk 'To Teachers', he strongly critiqued the fact that 'the child's life is subjected to the education factory, lifeless, colorless, dissociated from the context of the universe, within bare white walls staring like eyeballs of the dead' (as cited in Dasgupta, 2009, p. 108). He dropped-out of a number of English medium and Bengali medium schools. He was primarily home-schooled and later went on to establish his own co-educational school in rural tribal region of colonial Bengal, Shantiniketan.

The school was established as an alternative model of schooling attentive towards child's learning needs and abilities, contrary to the mainstream colonial factory-model of nineteenth-century schooling. Moreover, Tagore's 'socially inclusive school (also) aimed to bridge social divide across gender, race, ethnicity, tribe, caste and religion with a conscious pedagogy to educate the heart and the mind' (Mukherjee, 2014). This all-encompassing inclusive vision of schooling to bridge social divide stems from an important empathic and egalitarian theoretical position taken by Tagore, as Collins (2007, p. 80) writes:

> Tagore develops in his later writings and in his correspondence a particular type of anti-colonial agenda that evinces as much concern for the coloniser as for the colonised. He is unwilling to see the colonial situation as framed solely by the conflict of interest between the colonizer and the anti-colonial nationalist. Colonialism, Tagore would later argue, has been responsible for the subjugation of not only colonised peoples, but also Western civilisation itself, for it is colonialism that has led it away from its highest ideals. Resistance to colonialism should take the form of remedying the laws of both coloniser and colonised. It is this theoretical position, as well as Tagore's personal involvement in realising such goals, that makes him such a significant figure; both in terms of the intellectual history of colonialism and for the purposes of thinking about the relationship between East and West in the contemporary postcolonial period.

This was a very radical progressive philosophy within a colonial context of domination and discrimination, as it has been observed by several scholars in recent years (Dasgupta, 1998, 2013; Ghosh et al., 2010; Nussbaum, 2006, 2010; O'Connell, 2010). It expressed Tagore's ability to empathize also with plight of the colonizer/oppressor, as he considered relationships of domination were harmful for both the one who dominates and the other who is dominated. Hence, he emphasized egalitarian relationships as against dominating power relationships. This egalitarian relational principle was also embedded in his pedagogic project. One of the most critical readers of Tagore's work, Hogan (2003), used a Sanskrit and Bengali word 'sahrdaya'[13] to describe Tagore, since he was thinking and writing about equal human rights (manusher odhikar[14]) within the colonial Indian context of domination even prior to the international legal convention on human rights as Spivak (2002) suggested.

In the 'Pedagogy of the Heart' Paulo Freire (1998) wondered, 'if the majority of progressives had already understood that social transformation only really takes place when most of society takes ownership of it and takes the initiative to expand its social radius of acceptance' and the fact that, '(w)hen transformation is more or less imposed and its implementation is not followed by any effort or explanation about its reason for being, what results is blind obedience, immobilization, passivity, and fear. It may also lead, someday, to uprising' (p. 275). As Freire's 'intellectual forerunner' (Ghosh et al., 2010) within the Indian context, Tagore understood similar need to expand the 'social radius of acceptance' through socially inclusive democratic education.

This need to expand the 'social radius of acceptance' inside the school for its ripple effect outside in the society was also understood by the former principal of Delphine Hart School and some of the staff in the school, who came from inside the Jesuitess order and outside the order from indigenous Brahmo model of schooling established by Tagore's ancestors. An acute awareness of historic injustices and exploitation marked the conversational interviews with each of the prime actors in the school, who lead the inclusive transformation of the school since the 1979. This is overtly evident from the following quote from an interview:

> Everywhere you go you have the same big schools- these big elite schools. Everywhere! You don't find any place without them. And, everyone feathering the nest of well-off kids and then those kids will go on to later become leaders of the country and possibly bigger exploiters than those that were there already. I mean why all this exploitation continues? ... Because, the people who are doing it are coming from that same insensitive class, because they have never been sensitized as children.
>
> - Sister Valentine

Such a deep awareness of systemic social injustices by prime actors in the school because of their 'embodied' experiences coupled with a range of historic, cultural and political influences lead the school to conceptualize its distinct philosophy of engagement for the upliftment of the 'subalterns' of the local community. It also helped the former school Principal, Sister Valentine along with few other teachers in the school to design a relational values-education curriculum titled 'We are the World' in ten-part series based on a balanced approach towards heart and head values drawing on the principles of 'Golden Rule' from all major Indian religions, including Hinduism, Islam, Sikhism, Jainism, Judaism and Christianity. The curriculum is critical about different kinds of socioeconomic inequalities within the contemporary Indian society and deals with issues such as discrimination against girl child, caste-based discrimination and religious discrimination. In order to teach this curriculum, they also developed a five-step reflective teaching methodology involving both individual and group activities. This curriculum has now been adapted as the official Human Rights curriculum in the region and being disseminated to other schools. This values-based approach of Delphine Hart School has been studied and theorized by Bajaj (2011) along with the work of some other schools in India as Human Rights Education for transformative social action with an underlying 'radical politics of inclusion and social justice'.

Tagore was also extremely critical about the ills of indigenous Indian society during colonial times, just as he was critical about imperialism. Hence, he set out to reform education by establishing his own school where children's 'minds (will be) without fear'[15], and they would learn from the spiritual, artistic and scientific traditions of both eastern and western civilizations. Tagore prioritized a more ecologically conscious child-centred pedagogy for educating world-minded citizens in his school in rural Shantiniketan back in the early twentieth-century colonial India; as against commercialism, imperialism and blind nationalism (Bannerji, 2016; Dasgupta, 2009; Mukherjee, 2014; O'Connell 2010). Dasgupta (2013) writes: 'Rabindranath was seeking a world which has moved on from nationalism, patriotism, statism, and also capitalism- capitalism, because of his insistence on the best technology for Viswa-Bharati without the greed of profit ... Indeed, my research on a history of Shantiniketan-Sriniketan-Viswa Bharati has led me to believe that this education was a vision and an exercise in inclusion and variety, with its driving faith in the idea of a civilizational 'meeting' of the world's races for an intercultural dialog crafted through knowledge of history and the arts' (pp. 280–281). This humanist philosophy of education and vision for intercultural understanding is best expressed in Tagore's essay 'The Poet's School' in 1929:

> The minds of children today are almost deliberately made incapable of understanding other people with different languages and customs. The result is that later, they hurt one another out of ignorance and suffer the worst form of the blindness of the age ... I have tried to save our children from such aberrations, and here the help of friends from the West, with their sympathetic hearts, has been of the greatest service.

Conceptualizing Inclusive Pedagogy

Education by nature is a relational process according to Tagore. The child learns best through his relationship with teacher, peers and the environment. Hence, creating a socially inclusive education system involving intercultural education and paying attention towards the individual learning needs of every child was most important according to Tagore. As stated earlier in this article, this relational philosophy of education

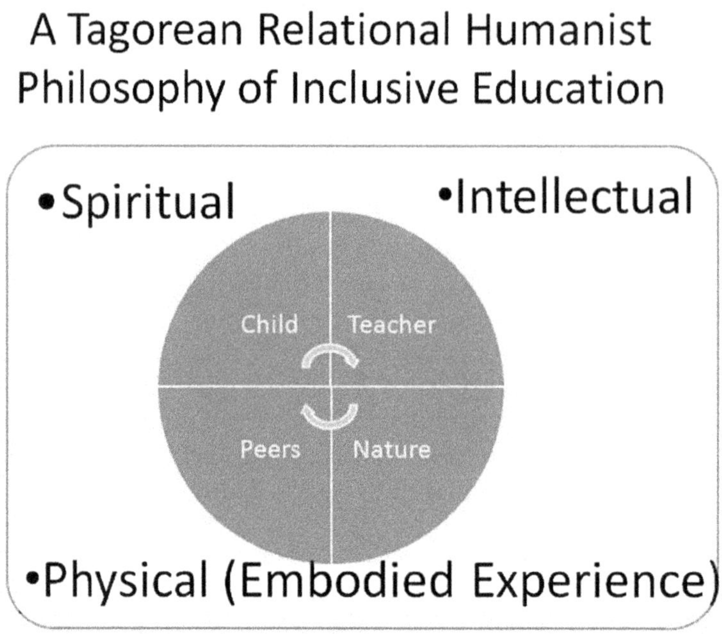

Figure 1: Tagore's relational humanist philosophy of inclusive education

emerged out of Tagore's own schooling experience as a child, as well as his subjective observations of the world around him as a child and as an adult during colonial India. As a 'rooted cosmopolitan'[16], Tagore believed in the interconnectivity of life on earth. He also knew that the only way to move beyond parochial nationalism especially within the colonial context and all kinds of discrimination based on nationality, gender, race, ethnicity, caste, class, etc. was through inclusive education.

Tagore was also extremely critical of the mechanization of the teaching–learning process during colonial India and emphasized that it was important to reconnect the head and the heart, since the child learns best through a relational process and physical activity. He wrote—'If we at all understand the needs of the present day, we must see that any new schools founded by us fulfill the following conditions: that their courses are both lively and varied, and nourish the heart as well as the intellect; that no disunity or discord disrupts the minds of our young; and that education does not become something for those few hours when they are at school' (Tagore, 1906 cited in Dasgupta, 2009, p. 114). According to Tagore, the child is relationally connected with the peer, teacher and the natural environment. Hence, the teaching–learning process should always take this into account. Any disruption or discord in these relationships is bound to affect the child's learning. Similarly, he saw the child's spiritual, intellectual and physical embodied self are also interconnected (see Figure 1). Hence, education should nourish all these aspects of the child's ontological being for holistic development, so that education becomes a life-long process and not limited to the few hours in the school.

Similar vision of education involving the education of the heart and the mind of students can be found in the 1971 constitution of the Jesuitess institute in India, which specifically stated that:

> Our goal is to form women alive to the needs of our world, with the knowledge which gives them power to act, and motivated by the love which gives them purpose and wisdom in their action. The education of girls from every social background has to be undertaken so that there can be produced not only women of refined talents but those great souled persons who are so desperately needed by our times. (p. 29)

A 1991 booklet on the school's vision, philosophy and policy further states that the progressive policies of the school 'followed naturally from our philosophy'. (p. 10) This philosophy of the school as stated in a school publication after a meditation retreat held at Dhyan Ashram, Calcutta, also reads very similar to the ideals of Christian liberation theology which grew in Latin America:

> We recognize and strongly affirm that the special thrust of our Institute becomes credible in India today when our schools are centers where a preferential love of the poor is lived out both in attitudes and structures. In cherishing the most deprived of His people, and enabling them to take their place with dignity among the others our schools become places where truly the Glory of God is manifested. (p. 8–9)

A deep concern for the poor 'subaltern' population and rising inequality within the indigenous society of colonial India can be also observed in Tagore's essays, stories, novels and also artistic poetic writings. The following quote from Tagore expresses this concern in the most eloquent way and critiques the dominant cultural practices of chanting and singing within the larger Indian society as superficial, rather than spiritual:

> Leave this chanting and singing and telling of beads!
> Whom do you worship in this lonely dark corner of a temple with doors all shut?
> Open your eyes and see your God is not before you!
> He is there where the tiller is tilling the hard ground and where the path maker is breaking stones.
> He is with them in sun and in shower, and his garment is covered with dust.
>
> -Tagore as translated from Bengali by Amartya Sen (2011)[17]

Tagore's critical awareness about increasing inequality during colonial India and culturally embedded social problems of the elites of Indian society spiritually disconnected from the suffering masses inspired him to build his own school in rural tribal Shantiniketan, rather than in his native city of Calcutta.

Within the extremely hierarchical and socioeconomic class, caste, gender and religion divided Indian society, where indigenous hierarchies got further reified because of new hierarchies born out of the rigid social class divided Victorian England, most children coming from well-off families (particularly studying in English-medium missionary schools) generally never touch the lives of poor children, unless they go into their houses as domestic servants, who are often treated very badly like slaves. By bringing these children into the heart of the school, by making them peers to socialize with children from well-off families, making them stand up and lead assemblies in front of other school children; the inclusive pedagogic approach of Delphine Hart School began breaking down all barriers. Since middleclass children, their parents and school staff became active stakeholders for the education of the marginalized; people began to see that these poor children are just the same as everybody else. Moving beyond the 'deficit ideology' often used to rationalize the failure of the marginalized, they began to see that these children only lacked the opportunity, social network and mentoring which children from well-off families receive through family.

The most striking element of conceptualizing such an inclusive pedagogy to educate the heart and the mind of children is that the development was organic and bottom-up. The policy changes in the school were led by a long-serving empathic school Principal, who served the institution for over 30 years. However, its demand came from students and several school staff following the rape of a little homeless girl outside the gates of the school, despite strong opposition from a section of school staff and parents. Moreover, the community-oriented personal values of the school principal coming from an impoverished background of rural Ireland during World War I was also a major driving force for change as it is also evident from the following quote:

> I grew up in Ireland. During my very early years the war in Europe was raging in the 1939–1940. I saw the Jewish children being smuggled out to Ireland. I saw condition they were in. And, Ireland was not an affluent country. It was a very poor country. During the winter there in 1940s when there was snow on the ground and it was bitterly cold, I sat with children who were without shoes beside me in the desk .... So when I see poor men here carrying heavy load, I see my own people.

The above quote is also a good example of the power of human empathy which can override differences based on race, nationality and social class location. I argue here that the last sentence in the above quote from the former school Principal express similar 'sahrdaya' sentiments which characterized much of Tagore's literary writings and also pedagogic work as argued by Hogan (2003).

Conclusion

Sachs (2014) writes, 'Sustainable Development targets three broad goals for society: economic development, social inclusion and environmental sustainability ... The goal of social inclusion is unfinished business in almost all parts of the world' (p. 219). While discussing the exclusion people experience around the world because of gender, race, indigenous identity and sexual orientation. he also highlights the fact that 'in modern economies, class is another possible barrier to social inclusion' (p. 220). The bottom-up organic model for social inclusion across class barriers led by social action of young middleclass girls therefore appear to be a good 'resource of hope', as Raymond Williams (1989) had argued. It is evident from this case study research that such a model of education can organically emerge within specific contexts led by community needs, youth social action and supportive school leadership. The historic colonial elitist design can be also changed through more democratic pedagogic models attentive of the diverse needs of learners and diversity of student body. However, since schools as social institutions are generally in a state of change 'driven by social, cultural and economic shifts and policy agendas.' (Thomson, Lingard, & Wrigley, 2012), sustainability of such a model is a big challenge as, I have observed through the process of my own research-related fieldwork (Mukherjee, 2015).

Even Tagore's inclusive school in Shantiniketan has a chequered history as observed by Radice (2010), and it remained towards the outer-fringes of the mainstream modern Indian education system, which emerged during British colonial times. How to sustain democratic inclusive pedagogic models based on philosophies of engagement to educate the heart and the mind across social divide for sustainable development? This is probably the most important question in the twenty-first century. However, the case study school and its conception of inclusive education show that local needs can inspire the establishment of inclusive schooling environment driven by supportive school leadership to educate the hearts and the minds of children. It shows that it is possible to conceptualize inclusive pedagogies through intercultural dialog and engagement with 'philosophy of context' and 'southern theory' arising out of the complex colonial encounters in the global south.

Disclosure statement

No potential conflict of interest was reported by the author.

Notes

1. Shantiniketan meaning 'abode of peace' was located in the rural tribal region of the Birbhum district of undivided colonial Bengal. It is now in the Birbhum district of the state of West Bengal, India.
2. The name of the school and research participants has been anonymized following the research ethics protocol of the University of Melbourne.
3. In recent times, Indian scholars have debated over the exact cause of the famine, though Joseph Lelyveld quotes economist Amartya Sen's (2010) reply to the editorial debate in The New York Review of Books to suggests that it was actually 'British imperial policy of confusion and callousness, which had disastrous consequences' See: http://www.nybooks.com/articles/archives/2011/feb/24/bengal-famine/
4. Most British and Indian Historians consider the freedom movement against colonial rule in India began with the Revolt of 1857. See: http://www.bbc.co.uk/history/british/victorians/indian_rebellion_01.shtml
5. The particular Catholic order of Nuns is generally known as the Jesuitess, since their founding Mother superior wanted to follow the scholarly Society of Jesus for men, the Jesuits.
6. See: literature on 'poor white' community during British India by Arnold (1979), Hawes (1996) and Stoler (1989).
7. Girls from scheduled caste, scheduled tribe, Muslim and backgrounds of disability are some of the most excluded children within the Indian schooling context, according to macro statistical data (both national and international). See India Exclusion Report 2014.

8. This cultural practice within the colonial Indian context has been analyzed at length by Spivak (1988) from a feminist perspective in her seminal essay—Can the subaltern Speak? While postcolonial ethnohistorian Chakrabarty (2007) has critiqued the transition of the woes of women as 'suttee' and widows from the private to the public sphere during colonial times as the 'birth' of the modern colonial subject.
9. See: Brahmo Samaj meaning Reformist Society http://www.thebrahmosamaj.net/history/history.html
10. 'Southern Theory' is a sociological term established by Connell (2007), who argued for the inadequacy of applying theoretical formulations from Northern European countries to analyse sociological problems and data from Southern postcolonial countries.
11. The name Upanishad has been variously interpreted. Many claim that it is a compound Sanskrit word Upa-ni-shad, signifying 'sitting at the feet or in the presence of a teacher'; while according to other authorities it means 'to shatter' or 'to destroy' the fetters of ignorance.
12. See: http://www.tagoreweb.in/Render/ShowContent.aspx?ct=Stories&bi=4A57AB73-A4A0-40D5-551D-9502E9CD11FD&ti=4A57AB73-A4A0-4FB5-251D-9502E9CD11FD
13. A 'sahridaya' person is someone who can feel for other people by emotionally being in the other person's shoes. However, these feeling and emotions are not irrational, since a 'sahridaya' person shares deep feelings with another person based on knowledge. See Abhinavagupta (1990) as cited by Hogan (2003).
14. See: Spivak (2002, p. 29) The Bengali word 'Manush' means human and 'odhikar' means rights.
15. See: Tagore's famous poem from his Nobel winning volume of poems 'Gitanjali'- Where the mind is without fear: http://allpoetry.com/poem/8516621-Where-The-Mind-Is-Without-Fear-by-Rabindranath-Tagore
16. This is how Purkayastha (2003) has read Tagore drawing on Kwame Anthony Appiah (1996) definition of the term, as someone who was rooted in his own cultural identity as a Bengali son of Mother India.
17. See: http://www.newrepublic.com/article/books/magazine/89649/rabindranath-tagore

References

Arnold, D. (1979). European orphans and vagrants in India in the nineteenth century. *The Journal of Imperial and Commonwealth History, 7*, 104–127.

Bajaj, M. (2011a). *Schooling for social change: The rise and impact of human rights education in India*. New York, NY: Continuum Publishing.

Bajaj, M. (2011b). Human rights education: ideology, location, and approaches. *Human Rights Quarterly, 33*, 481–508.

Bannerji, H. (2016). A transformational pedagogy: Reflections on Rabindranath's project of decolonisation. In Sangeeta Datta & Subhoranjan Dasgupta (Eds.), *Tagore the world as his nest* (pp. 24–60). Kolkata: Jadavpur University Press.

Bara, J. (2000). Christian missionaries and popular education in India, 1910–40. *Indian Social Science Review: A multidisciplinary Journal, 2*, 301–333.

Bellenoit, H. (2014). Education, missionaries and the Indian Nation, c. 1880–1920. In Parimala.V. Rao (Ed.), *New perspectives in the history of Indian education* (pp. 176–195). New Delhi: Orient Black Swan.

Berryman, P. (1987). *Liberation theology: Essential facts about the revolutionary movement in Latin America - and beyond*. New York, NY: Pantheon Books.

Besley, T., & Peters, M. A. (2011). Introduction. Interculturalism, ethnocentrism and dialogue. *Policy Futures in Education, 9*(1), 1–11.

Bhattacharya, K. (2013). *Rabindranath Tagore: Integrating adventure of ideas and innovative practices in education*. Springer Briefs on Key Thinkers in Education. Wien: Springer.

Brown, R. M. (1993). *Liberation theology: An introductory guide*. Louisville: Westminster/John Knox Press.

Carnoy, M. (1974). *Education as cultural imperialism*. New York, NY: David McKay.

Chakrabarty, D. (2007). *Provincializing Europe: Postcolonial thought and historical difference*. Princeton, NJ: Princeton University Press.

Chattopadhay, T. (2015). Bridging the social divides: A school-based model from India. *International Journal of Sociology and Social Policy, 35*, 222–238.

Chen, K. (2010). *Asia as method: toward deimperialization*. Durham, NC: Duke University Press.

Clarke, S. (1998). *Dalits and christianity: Subaltern religion and liberation theology in India*. New Delhi: Oxford University Press.

Collins, M. (2007). History and the postcolonial: Rabindranath Tagore's reception in London, 1912–1913. *International Journal of the Humanities, 4*, 71–83.

Colmcille, M., I.B.V.M. (1968). *First the blade; history of the I.B.V.M. (Loreto) in India, 1841–1962*. Calcutta: Firma K. L. Mukhopadhyay.

Connell, R. (2007). *Southern theory: The global dynamics of knowledge in social science*. Crows Nest, NSW: Allen & Unwin

Dasgupta, U. (1998). Tagore's educational experiments in Shantiniketan and Sriniketan 1910–1941. In S. Bhattacharya (Ed.), *The contested terrain: Perspectives on education in India* (pp. 265–274). New Delhi: Orient Longman

Dasgupta, U. (Ed.). (2009). *Tagore: Selected writings on education and nationalism*. New Delhi: Oxford University Press.

Dasgupta, U. (2013). Rabindranath's experiments with education, community and nation at his Shantiniketan institutions. In S. Dasgupta & C. Guha (Eds.), *Tagore- at home in the world* (pp. 279–290). Los Angeles: Sage.

Doggett, R. (2005). Enabling education for girls: The loreto day school, Sealdah, India. In S. Aikmanm & E. Unterhalter (Eds.), *Beyond access: Transforming policy and practice for gender equality in education* (pp. 227–244). Oxford: Oxfam GB.

Freire, P. (1998). Pedagogy of the Heart. In A. M. A. Freire & D. Macedo (Eds.), *The Paulo Freire reader* (pp. 265–282). New York, NY: Continuum.

Ghosh, R. (2015). Caught in the cross traffic: Rabindranath Tagore and the trials of child education. *Comparative Education Review, 59*, 399–419.

Ghosh, R., Naseem, A., & Vijh, A. (2010). Tagore and education: Gazing beyond the colonial cage. In A. Abdi (Ed.), *Decolonizing philosophies of education* (pp. 59–72). Rotterdam: Sense Publishers.

Greene, E. (1995). *From dirty streets to rainbows*. Dublin: The Pontifical University of Maynooth.

Guha, M. (2013). Education in a tagorean perspective. *International Journal of Humanities and Social Science Invention, 2*, 35–41.

Harris, M., & Johnston, M. A. (2010). Values-based leadership: At the heart of sustaining school reform and improvement. In S. G. Huber, R. C. Saravanabhavan, & S. Hader-Popp (Eds.), *School leadership: International perspectives* (pp. 145–160). Dordrecht: Springer.

Hawes, C. (1996). *Poor relations: The making of a eurasian community in British India 17730–1833*. Surrey: Curzon Press.

Hogan, P. (2003). Introduction: Tagore and the ambivalence of commitment. In P. C. Hogan & L. Pandit (Eds.), *Rabindranath Tagore: Universality and tradition* (pp. 9–28). Madison: Fairleigh Dickinson University Press; London: Associated University Presses

Jalan, R. V. (1976). *Tagore- his educational theory and practice and its impact on Indian education* (Doctoral Thesis). University of Florida. Retrieved from http://www.archive.org/details/tagorehiseducati00jala

Jessop, T. (1998). *A model of best practice at Loreto day school*. Sealdah, Kolkata: Occasional Paper no. 1 DFID.

Kumar, C. (2009). Migration and refugee issue between India and Bangladesh. *Scholar's View: A New Way of Thinking* (Biannual Publication of the Center for Defence Studies Research & Development), *1*, 64–82

MHRD. (2011). *Sarva Shikshya abhiyan: Framework for implementation*. New Delhi: Government of India.

Mukherjee, H. B. (2013). *Education for fullness: A study of the educational thought and experiment of Rabindranath Tagore*. New Delhi: Routledge.

Mukherjee, M. (2014). The possibility of a Southern theory of inclusive education in 'An Other Tongue'. In *The Australian sociological association annual conference Social theory thematic group*. Challenging Identities, Institutions and Communities. Retrieved from https://www.tasa.org.au/wp-content/uploads/2014/12/Mukherjee.pdf

Mukherjee, M. (2015). From missionary to new middle-class schooling in the era of global capitalism. In J. Sprague (Ed). *Globalization and Transnational Capitalism in Asia and Oceania* (pp. 214–228). New York: Routledge

Mukherjee-Reed, A. (2008). *Human development and social power: Perspectives from South Asia*. New York, NY: Routledge.

Nolan, M. J. (2008). *The enterprising life of Dr Henry Backhaus*. Bendigo: Bendigo Pioneer.

Nussbaum, M. (2006). *Education for democratic citizenship*. The Netherlands: Lecture Delivered on the Occasion of the Awarding of the Degree of Doctor Honoris Causa at the Institute of Social Studies. Retrieved from http://www.iss.nl/fileadmin/ASSETS/iss/Documents/Academic_publications/nussbaum_text.pdf

Nussbaum, M. (2010). *Not for profit: Why democracy needs the humanities* (Martha C. Nussbaum). Princeton, NJ: Princeton University Press.

O'Connell, K. (2003). Siksar Herfer: Education out of Whack. In P. C. Hogan & L. Pandit (Eds.), *Rabindranath Tagore: Universality and tradition* (pp. 65–84). Madison, NJ: Fairleigh Dickinson University Press; London: Associated University Presses.

O'Connell, K. (2010). 'Rabindranath Tagore: Envisioning humanistic education at Shantiniketan (1902–1922)', The topic: The international Tagore. The problem special issue. *International Journal on Humanistic Ideology*, *3*, 15–42.

Peters, M. A. (2012). Editorial: Educational research and the philosophy of context. *Educational Philosophy and Theory*, *44*, 793–800. doi:10.1111/j.1469-5812.2012.00845.x.

Pridmore, J. (2009). The poet's school and the parrot's cage: The educational spirituality of Rabindranath Tagore. *International Journal of Children's Spirituality*, *14*, 355–367.

Purkayastha, B. (2003). Contesting the boundaries between home and the world: Tagore and the construction of citizenship. In Patrick Colm Hogan & Lalita Pandit (Eds)., *Rabindranath Tagore: Universality and tradition* (pp. 49–65). London: Associated University Press.

Radice, W. (2010). Never not an educator: Tagore as a poet teacher. *Asiatic*, *4*, 41–51.

Reinke, L. (2004). Globalization and local indigenous education in Mexico. *International Review of Education.*, *50*, 483–496.

Sachs, J. D. (2014). *The age of sustainable development*. New York, NY: Columbia University Press.

Saha, P. (2013). Singing Bengal into a nation: Tagore the colonial cosmopolitan? *Journal of Modern Literature*, Special Issue - Aesthetic Politics—Revolutionary and Counter Revolutionary (Winter 2013) 36, 1–24.

Samuel, F. A. (2011). Educational vision from two continents: What Tagore adds to the Deweyan perspective. *Educational Philosophy and Theory, 43*, 1161–1174.

Sen, A. (2011). *Poetry and reason: Why Rabindranath Tagore still matters*. Retrieved from https://newrepublic.com/article/89649/rabindranath-tagore

Seth, S. (2007). *Subject lessons: The Western education of colonial India*. Durham: Duke University Press.

Spivak, G. C. (1988). Can the subaltern speak? In C. Nelson & L. Grossberg (Eds). *Marxism and the interpretation of culture* (pp. 271–313). Baskinstoke: Macmillan Education

Spivak, G. C. (1994). Bonding in difference. In A. Arteaga (Ed.), *An other tongue: Nation and ethnicity in the linguistic borderlands* (pp. 273–286). Durham: Duke University Press.

Spivak, G. (2002). Ethics and politics in Tagore, Coetzee, and certain scenes of teaching. *Diacritics, 32*, 17–31.

Stoler, A. L. (1989). Making empire respectable: The politics of race and sexual morality in 20th-century colonial cultures. *American Ethnologist, 16*, 634–660.

Tagore, R. (1892). Shikshar Herfer. In *Shikshya, Shantiniketan*, Visva-Bharati, 17–19.

Tagore, R. (1906). The Problem of Education. In *Towards Universal Man, 1961* (pp. 67–82). Bombay: Asia.

Tagore, R. (1912/2000). *Apoman, Gitanjali song 108*. (Joe Winter, Trans.). London: Anvil Press

Tagore, R. (1917). *'My School', Personality*. London: MacMillan.

Tagore, R. (1929). A poet's school. In *Towards Universal Man, 1961* (pp. 285–301). Bombay: Asia.

Tagore, S. (2008). Tagore's conception of cosmopolitanism: A reconstruction. *University of Toronto Quarterly, 77*, 1070–1084. doi:10.3138/utq.77.4.1070.

Thomson, P., Lingard, B., & Wrigley, T. (2012). Reimagining school change: The necessity and reasons for hope. In T. Wrigley, P. Thomson, & B. Lingard (Eds.), *Changing schools: Alternative ways to make a world of difference* (pp. 1–14). New York, NY: Routledge

Vavrus, F., & Bartlett, L. (2006). Comparatively knowing: Making a case for the vertical case study. *Current Issues in Comparative Education, 8*, 95–103.

Williams, R. (1989). *Resources of hope: Culture, democracy, socialism* (Raymond Williams; edited by Robin Gable; with an introduction by Robin Blackburn). London: Verso.

No-Self, Natural Sustainability and Education for Sustainable Development

Chia-Ling Wang

Abstract

This article explores the significance of sustainability and several ways in which education for sustainable development (ESD) can be considered. It presents several issues related to the theories of sustainability and ESD, which are generated based on a firm concept of anthropocentrism. ESD has been used for developing a scientific understanding of the world and is expected to effectively address the environmental damage facing humans. However, this is a narrow view of sustainability, through which learners do not gain an authentic understanding of nature. If the phenomenon of ecological interdependence is true, a non-anthropocentric stance of sustainability is the actual representation required for ESD teaching. Ecological wisdom in Buddhist philosophy indicates that natural sustainability corresponds to human living in harmony with the natural environment, an insight derived particularly from the Buddhist concept of the no-self. Instead of denying the existence of 'I', the no-self is the loss of self-preoccupation. This notion highlights the non-dual relation between the self and this world. If I am I and nature is nature, then human sustainability differs from natural sustainability. Only when I am nature and nature is I can natural sustainability translate into human sustainability. This state presents actual sustainability for humans. Regarding ESD, it can be achieved by coming to nature, and learning to see nature in ourselves. As nature does, it comes to all beings, manifesting itself in all beings.

Introduction

The notion of 'sustainability' and related strategies has been discussed in the past three decades under worsening environmental crises. Certain people prefer using the term, 'sustainable development', rather than sustainability. Sustainability has various definitions. As defined in the *Brundtland Report* (World Commission on Environment and Development, 1987), sustainability is the systematic, long-term use of natural resources that can be available for future generations. Development is encouraged for progress in both economic and social aspects, without having to destroying environmental resources. Based on this description, sustainability is considered from the viewpoint of social justice, ethical acceptance, moral fairness and economic soundness. Sustainability generally refers to long-term prospects with ecological, political, economic and societal implications. It is a dynamic process that extends to the global level (Filho, Manolas, & Pace, 2009). Education plays a central role in promoting sustainable development. A UNESCO report (2012) released by the United Nations Conference on Sustainable Development defines ESD as follows:

> ESD is education for the future, for everyone to acquire the values, competencies, skills and knowledge that are necessary to shape sustainable development. It is essential to ensure a successful transition to green societies and economies. This calls for a reorientation of current formal and nonformal education at all level … ESD creates active and ecologically responsible citizens and consumers who are prepared to address the complex global and local challenges facing the world today, such as climate change. (UNESCO, 2012, p. 16)

According to this document, ESD is practiced with the goal of achieving green societies and economies. Its mission is to cultivate ecologically responsible citizens and consumers. The aim of ESD appeals to a sustainable society, with economic development resolving global ecological crises such as global warming, climate change, pollution and resources shortage. This general concept represents the functions of sustainability to people. However, when viewed broadly, as a way of life, ESD cannot be considered without including the relationship between humans and nature. Sustainable living is required for changing how we think of ourselves and for developing a more sustainable way of being in the world. Reorienting ourselves as 'being in and of the world' (Danvers, 2009) is essential to ESD.

Murray (2011) developed the 'sustainable self' as a personal approach to ESD, indicating that being 'unsustainable' is a habit that is not easily altered. Moving towards sustainable habits involves how we think, but changing our manner of thinking requires more time than expected. Therefore, he promoted six attributes (or qualities) that enable people to live with sustainability in mind. These attributes are awareness, motivation, empowerment, knowledge, skilful means and practice. Murray offered specific recommendations with detailed examples for obtaining these attributes, which are extremely helpful for ESD practice.

Murray's concept of achieving the aim of sustainability is valuable. Furthermore, I agree with Bonnett's claim that a metaphysical transformation is also required for an adequate response to our environmental predicaments (Bonnett, 2006). For Bonnett, this metaphysical transformation connects with an 'attitude of mind' towards nature. We need a metaphysical transformation in which the real wisdom of coexisting with nature can be realised. The metaphysical fact that the rule of natural movement can never be transgressed should also be understood. A positive attitude guides an ecologically sustainable view, which can solve ecological crises. The main problem of unsustainability in modern society is that people have the wrong attitude about getting along with nature. This leads to ecological destruction and generates tense relations between humans and nature.

In the Western philosophical tradition, Descartes distinguished between the non-physical human mind and the physical body. Christian instruction has perpetuated the notion of dualism (e.g. God/humanity, spirit/matter, good/evil and heaven/earth). These dichotomies lead to a fragmented view of relations between human and nature and inform the modern notion that nature is part of the material world; it is to be conquered and utilised to benefit human welfare. In classic Asian philosophy, the relation between humans and nature is regarded in a different manner. All beings in nature are embedded in an organic oneness. In my view, this holistic thinking regarding living in nature comprises valuable wisdom for exploring the significance of sustainable human living. I have found that Buddhist philosophy offers a rich discussion on the role of ecology in the profound relation between the self and the universal, which may typify a wise attitude for leading a green lifestyle, leading to the balanced development of all creatures and maintaining an ecologically sustainable world. Regarding an individual approach to sustainability, Buddhism provides valuable thought to promote ESD and furthermore to 'move our action from ego to eco—to become Naturally Smart' (Clarke, 2012). The Buddhist concept of the *no-self* shows a profound wisdom for realising the sustainable self. The no-self is the notion of the self that is fully compatible with a natural progression. The individual can use this authentic approach to move towards the sustainability of being-in-this-world. I attempt to elaborate on the no-self and analyse its ontological foundation of non-dualism to reveal a significant aspect of being in nature

This article first presents several issues in ESD discourse that are caused by a firm concept of anthropocentrism. Their positions might hinder sustainable practices in education. Afterward, I adopt ecological concepts from Buddhist philosophy by considering an approach to living in harmony with the natural environment. I suggest that the no-self can foster sustainable relations between us and nature. Its significance is compatible with the ultimate purpose of ecological sustainability. In closing, I offer recommendations in considering implications of ESD.

The Notion of Anthropocentrism-Based Sustainability

Many approaches have been used to examine sustainability (or sustainable development). It is regarded as a conceptually problematic term for which various interpretations have been offered. The meaning of sustainability is difficult to be pinned down. Shiva (1992) indicated that the 'development' in sustainable development was based on the growth of the market economy. She distinguished between two types of sustainability approaches. Most policies towards sustainability concern 'sustainability in the marketplace' rather than 'sustainability in nature'. This approach to sustainability is oxymoronic because it negatively affects both the environment's natural progression and human living in nature. Stables (2013) found a conceptual conflict in the notion of sustainable development. For Stables (2013), this term is an oxymoron: '"Sustainability" implies lack of change, whereas "development" implies change' (p. 182). He elaborates further:

> 'Sustainable development' is a piece of political rhetoric designed to act as a regulative ideal to guide our actions in response to this threat, but it is difficult to see how it can have any very profound effect. (Stables, 2013, p. 183)

According to Stables, sustainability is more of a political slogan than a concept based on logical reasoning. It is a hypothesis on existence for sustaining life on Earth, but a proposition that can never be achieved in reality. Our lives are limited, a subject discussed in literature, in which many poets mourn the death. For Stables, permanence can be pursued only by appealing to spiritual experiences in the arts and humanities. Stables observed that the crisis of unsustainability prompts human action for change. Much rhetoric on sustainable development is governed by a utilitarian logic of means-ends instrumentalism for improving unsustainable conditions. However, such expectations generally lead to naught.

Bonnett offered his critique of educational policies for sustainable development. He reviewed the rationale behind the general stance towards ESD. In his view, the logic of ESD has been inspired by an overweening technoscientific paradigm for immediate gratification and short-term human gains. As a metaphysics of mastery, implicit scientism is employed for satisfying material well-being through the channel of sustainable development (Bonnett, 2013b), a stance observable in certain ESD practices and reflected in its instrumental values. For example, ESD is applied to improving schools or to promoting national economic competition by developing green technologies (Bonnett, 2013a). Differing from these ideas, Bonnett proposed a non-instrumental concept of development as a goal for humanity. He preferred viewing the essence of sustainability as an 'attitude of mind' (Bonnett, 2006, p. 274). A mind for sustainability involves human openness, responsiveness and a responsibility for things in nature (which includes creatures and non-creatures). Bonnett explained that this differs from 'sustaining' the resources required for further purposes but is regarded 'as a concern to let things be (as they are in themselves)—to safeguard, to preserve, to conserve' (Bonnett, 2006, p. 274). In addition, he suggested an appropriate approach to ecological thinking regarding ESD. A holistic view includes social, economic and environmental factors, acting based on the systematic wisdom of the whole. Bonnett focuses on how people construct sustainable relations with nature. In his argument on ESD concepts, he provided a route for thinking of our basic stance towards the natural environment.

According to these critiques, the problem of sustainable development is that its goals are pervaded by a heavily instrumental and anthropocentric perspective. Human living conditions are considered to be of primary importance. Based on this viewpoint, ESD focuses on human development and develops a scientific understanding of this world. Moreover, it is expected to effectively resolve the environmental damage facing humans. However, this expectation reveals a narrow sense of sustainability, in which learners do not gain an authentic understanding of nature. If ecological interdependence is a natural phenomenon, a non-anthropocentric stance of sustainability is the actual representation that must be taught in ESD. In accordance with Bonnett's notion, which views 'sustainability as an attitude of mind', this would entail maintaining an open mind towards non-humans rather than guarding a closed mind by considering only ourselves.

Sustainability in Nature and the Nature of Sustainability

Sustainability in nature has never been a problem. Nature inherently functions in a sustainable and harmonious manner. All creatures live under its care for generations. The crisis of unsustainability begins with human overexploitation, which destroys the natural inner balance, in turn presenting problems for human life. A contradiction results here: first, a large amount of human exploitation invades the tranquil natural environment; second, humans intend to solve these self-created problems without being aware that nature has its own rules in which humans are embedded. Po-Lin Chi is a well-known Taiwanese aerial photographer. He has taken more than 300,000 aerial images of Taiwan and continues to seek unique views at different latitudes to document the panorama. Similar to colourful scenic paintings, his photographic landscapes evoke aesthetic sensibilities. Many environmental detriments are also captured in his images. A person once asked him, 'Where is the most beautiful place in Taiwan?' He responded, 'The most beautiful place is the place where there are no human beings'. This is an extremely sombre response, which sadly indicates the natural suffering resulting from humans' ruthless treatment of the environment.

An examination of sustainability concerns not only human sustainability but also involves an interrelated system that includes all living beings in nature. In this interdependent ecological system, human values are not the guide. Nature has its own supreme and omnipresent laws (*dao* in Chinese Daoism) for operating all creation. This law sustains humans and all other beings. How humans fit into natural law is the essence of sustainability for humans, which can be a good lesson for ESD. Interpreting the 'development' in sustainable development is improper when equating economic development or scientific improvement with the environment. Nevertheless, an authentic understanding is warranted, in which richer interrelations are developed between humans and humans, humans and the environment, humans and various creatures, and even humans and diverse non-creatures. These interrelations can be viewed as 'an ethic that can sustain the best that is in us while empowering us to live in harmony with the natural environment' (Newton, 2003, p. 2). In its development, humans renew themselves through a dynamic progression; sustainable living is thus accomplished. However, how can this sustainable living be established? I explore this notion by drawing from Buddhist ecological wisdom. A possible harmonious integration between humans and nature is discussed based on the concept of no-self.

The Concept of the No-Self in Buddhism

Before discussing Buddhist concept of the no-self, a related concept requires clarification. From a Buddhist ecological perspective, no self-existent thing exists. Everything is dependent on everything else, and things are empty of their own being. Their being is dependent on everything. They do not have an essence of their own. Being empty allows various configurations to occur. Because of emptiness, things can 'own their own being, to be themselves by themselves' (King, 2009, p. 46). The 'perfection of wisdom' in Buddhism involves realising this emptiness, in which all fixed beings and entities consciously constructed in our mind are 'undone'. Under this realisation, boundless openness and an extremely flexible mind can be generated.

The constitution of the self is identical to that of things. According to the Buddhist view, the essence of the self does not exist. The word 'I' typically refers to something that constitutes one's personal identity. However, the essence as the core of one's identity does not exist. This notion is called the no-self in Buddhism and can be understood from several perspectives (King, 2009, p. 19): first, humans are compound beings, composed of multiple thoughts, emotions and intentions. No single entity constitutes one's selfhood or is the basis for one's identity. Second, humans are beings who are always in progression, changing every moment. We are constructing ourselves based on the choices we make. Rather than in isolated circumstances, these choices are made in a great web of interdependence. Third, similar to all other things in this world, humans are conditioned by others and condition others in return.

No-self does not mean that 'I' does not exist but reminds us that we are constantly becoming 'other-than-we-were' (King, 2009, p. 20). When I consider, 'I am' in this moment, which becomes 'I was' in the following moment. The consciousness of 'I' is thus illusory; it is not something we can retain. The no-self approximates a spiritual level of selflessness, reminding us that humans should be free of the attitude of egotism. The human 'self' is neither the centre of the universe nor the ruler of its surroundings. All manipulations for securing the material conditions for existence are based on illusory intentions. There is neither a subject 'I' who can receive nor an object 'things' that can be received because nothing is substantial. The physical 'I' still exists; the notion that we should deny is a sense that clings to the ego. Therefore, the no-self is rather the 'loss of self-preoccupation' (Loy, 2003, p. 184) than the self dissolving in this world. Instead of the self-consciousness that we guard, the sense of self is what, on the contrary, we must forget. This self-forgetting 'allows the things of the world to "incorporate" me' (ibid.). The self and this world thus interpenetrate. The more one forgets the self, the deeper one involves in this world, which corresponds to the Buddhist practice of non-attachment. It is the end of clinging to the notion of 'I'. Buddhists believe that clinging to 'I' is the reason for the generation of psychospiritual suffering. This mistaken notion is also at the core of the problem of human condition (King, 2009).

No-self is a Buddhist deconstruction of the self, an ontological status of the self rather than a conceptual imagination. Buddhist philosophy suggests that people should be aware of this reality and change their cognition, habit and life according to this ontological fact, thereby achieving a goodness of life—a coherence with natural life. By exploring the reality of the no-self, one discovers the self. This genuine 'I' differs from the illusory 'I' based on self-consciousness.

A Relationship of Non-duality with Others

As the ego-self is expelled from the consciousness, the nature of the self emerges. Similar to how the no-self sees one's self, one can see things as they are in themselves. This is because of the absence of duality in the mind. No difference is made between the self and others. In this sense, there is no ownership, no control and no instrumental considerations. As in one's body, both the right hand and left hand belong to a single organic structure. They never intent to control each other, only to cooperate in an integrated manipulation. 'Letting things be' is how the no-self treats all beings. This is similar to the concepts by Heidegger and Bonnett, that we should not disrupt things in nature so that they can flourish. This notion manifests a spiritual practice of being with others, which can also be observed in Chinese Daoism. Daoism supports the concept of *non-action* for a wise attitude of being in this world. Non-action cannot be mistakenly interpreted as doing nothing, as shown in its surface meaning. On the contrary, it means that people should expend effort towards fulfilling human responsibilities, along with an attitude of working without receiving any reward. Non-action serves to manifest the significance of the no-self. If one raises actions with an ego-self, the actions are always performed for instrumental purposes in which realistic benefits are sought. However, non-action is completed with no desire. In the manner of nature flourishing all living beings, all actions are performed by the pure giving. Nature never wishes for any reward. This is the sound attitude for humans to conduct themselves and to treat others.

For Nhat Hanh (2008), the *Diamond Sutra* is the most ancient text on deep ecology. This scripture involves highly profound ecological wisdom. It reveals the non-duality of the self and this world. The no-self is deeply interpreted in this Mahayana classic. For instance, the *perfection of giving*, in which there is no giver, no receiver and no act of giving, is discussed in the *Diamond Sutra* (King, 2009). In reality, these three have not vanished, but the giver cannot have these three elements in mind when practicing the perfection of giving. If the three elements are embedded in the mind, one cannot be free of any conscious or subconscious thoughts of 'I' and 'you'. This concept of Buddhist charity is also highlighted by a sentence in the *Diamond Sutra*: 'If a Bodhisattva retains the notion of an ego, a personality, a being and a life, he is not a true Bodhisattva' (Nan, 2004, p. 55). Bodhisattva is the Buddhist virtuous status reserved for a person with great compassion and a sense of morality. The notion of a personality and a being are connected to those of society and humanity in modern language. According to Nan (2004), there are two types of notion regarding the ego. The first is the idea of separating living; that is, I am I, and you are you. The other type of ego is non-physical, which is the intention of those who want to achieve (e.g. a high status or social power) and become superior to others. When one has this aim, the notion of a personality and a being cannot avoid being incorporated into an ego-self. The fourth notion, 'a life', entails the lifespan (i.e. the desire that 'I' live a long and healthy life), which is the ultimate desire for most people. These four notions present the ego, in which a feeling of 'I' is grasped. Irrespective of the circumstance, these four notions are frequently packaged as one. This sentence states that a Bodhisattva should not distinguish between the self and others (including other beings, except from humans). As shown in this example of Buddhist virtue, if it is given, it is given. It is performed while being forgotten; having forgotten the notion of an ego, a personality, a being and a life, there is no intention of attaining them in return. As written in a poem, 'Events are like spring dreams, gone without a trace' (ibid.). Never selfish, nature gives birth to all things, yet it possesses nothing, which is the highest form of wisdom that humans can learn. From the perspective of this lesson from nature, when relating to others and attempting not to get caught, one thinks and acts in notions of a person, a being and a life. These notions are all empty in their being, which is occupied by nothing; however, if they reside in one's mind, complete wisdom cannot be manifested.

The No-Self and Sustainability

How does the no-self contribute to the thinking of sustainability? According to Buddhist non-dualism, no bifurcation can be drawn between humans and nature because all things are interdependent. Humans and nature are in a state of oneness. There is no difference between the no-self and the self. If an 'I' is not identified in the mind, the no-self and the self become identical. Humans are never this distinctive; a person is merely an integral part of nature. Following this line of non-duality, no dual notion of sustainability and non-sustainability can exist. Nature is permanently 'Being-as-it-is' (Suzuki, 2006, p. 286). Sustainability emerges because of human requirements. Paradoxically, human desire is also the source of unsustainability. Strategies for sustainability are derived from human fears of a limited lifespan and of deteriorating living space. However, these strategies do not address the core problems of sustainability. As shown in the warning in the *Diamond Sutra*, the desire of a lifespan is related to our persistence of the ego-self, identical to the ownership of space.

Both life and death are natural phenomena. In the natural movement of circulation, death creates opportunities for the living; it is an essential element of life. Conversely, the journey of life finally reaches its termination in death. Though there is a life–death differentiation in the notion of the lifespan, both life and death are caught in a constant process of natural sustainability. Similarly, the cells in human bodies must be renewed cyclically for healthy living. Regarding human growth, the death of an old notion allows new thoughts to emerge. Regarding concepts of sustainability, we can derive the essence of sustainability from nature, rather than seeking sustainability from an anthropocentric viewpoint. If nature itself is sustainable, then humans, as part of it, should be sustainable. However, this condition is attained only when humans and nature become integrated. An example of this concept is shown in a well-known Chinese metaphor: a mountain can be observed at three levels of awareness, ranging from shallow to deep. The first stage involves a sighting of a mountain. This first glimpse involves a superficial understanding of it. At the second stage, the mind doubts that the mountain was observed, suspicious of initially discerning a mountain. After observing additional scenes, one starts to dispute whether what one saw was actually a mountain, or whether it was part of some other experience because an understanding of the original observation is different from later experience. At the final stage, the doubt has been rectified by a life of many experiences. One eventually sees this mountain as a mountain, as it truly is. This mountain-watching metaphor is compatible with the three stages of realising this world in one's life, from a young age to middle age to old age. The Japanese Zen master Suzuki examined this analogy from the viewpoint of Zen and explained that the final stage can be regarded as follows:

> I am in Nature and Nature is in me. Not mere participation in each other, but a fundamental identity between the two. Hence, the mountains are mountains and the rivers are rivers; they are there before me. The reason I can see the mountains as mountains and the waters as waters is because I am in them and they are in me. (Suzuki, 2006, p. 284)

Suzuki revealed the notion of *interbeing* in this example. Nature is not separate from oneself. The mountains are actually mountains when assimilated into one's being, and one is absorbed into them. In this manner, for Suzuki, pure subjectivity is pure objectivity. Subject–object opposition does not exist, only the oneness between them. Instead of a human knowledge of nature, one sees nature as it really is. Our inner life is complete after merging into nature and becoming one with it. Because I discover my Being-as-I-am, I can see nature's Being-as-it-is. Both Being-as-I-am and Being-as-it-is are called s*uchness* in Buddhism. Suchness is the state of being as it is. In line with this notion, if I am I and nature is nature, my sustainability differs from natural sustainability. Only when I am nature and nature is I can natural sustainability be my sustainability. This state is real sustainability for humans.

Implications for ESD

In ESD policies, as Sterling (2009) indicated, we 'tend to devalue one side against the other (ecology against economics, nature against people, values against facts, etc.)' (p. 81). Instead, we must see all things in relation, rather than in opposition, to each other, which is an appropriate attitude for sustainable development. Certain thoughts of the discussed no-self may apply to ESD. A practice for liberating ourselves from dualistic thought, no-self thinking entails recognising our interdependence with others. Nature manifests supreme reality. It is the target we must live with and learn from. In nature, no rule of mutual opposition exists. This non-duality can transcend the limitations of physical structures, allowing the existence of all beings. In natural sustainability, there is no beginning and no end; everything is developing in its own becoming while experiencing interbeing with others. Regarding education, we can venture into nature while learning to see nature in ourselves. As nature does, it comes to all beings (include humans), manifesting itself in all beings.

Providing a good recommendation for educational practice, Bonnett (2009a) indicated that school must offer not only abstract and intellectual models but also opportunities for students to experience elements of nature. These experiences favourably affect students' attentiveness and their engagement in nature, by which 'a *mutual anticipation* (and invitation) of self and world is in play in which each is called forth' (Bonnett, 2009b, p. 32). This teaching is related to cultivating *ecological literacy*, as advocated by Orr (1992). Orr claims that one component of ecological literacy is a broad understanding of how people and societies are interrelated as well as associated with natural systems and how they might engage in these relations in a sustainable manner.

Mindfulness practice is a feasible approach to encouraging students' deep attention towards nature. The mindfulness movement has prospered over the past few decades. Jon Kabat-Zinn is its main figure, who developed a mindfulness-based stress reduction programme in the United States, in 1979. His work raises meaningful discussion on mindfulness. The application of mindfulness has achieved rapid success in schools for educational purposes. Mindfulness is rooted in the Buddhist tradition, in which bare attention and non-conceptual and non-judgemental awareness are central teachings (Hyland, 2015). Mindfulness is an effective manner of de-centring the self. Through mindfulness practices, individual habits and tendencies can be removed from the self. Because of the bare attention of the self-consciousness, the real attention of the inner true self and the outer environment is enhanced. A holistic view between humans and the environment is thus raised. This view includes a deep understanding of humans and nature being integral in a harmonious oneness. The educational purpose of ESD is to enhance the spiritual awareness that opens students' sensibility towards nature. Through awareness, compassion can be developed in treating all beings. Engaging in walking meditation in nature is also a practical manner of mindfulness for enlightening ecological wisdom, as exemplified by Thoreau's walks around Walden Pond (O'Donnell, 2015). Nothing needs to be thought of; thus, learners can enjoy the pleasure and release of being in nature. The real wisdom of natural sustainability is thus generated. ESD is perfected not by indoctrinating knowledge but by the self-awareness of human nature through realising the human–nature correlation.

Concluding Remarks

This article examined several controversies related to sustainability and sustainable development. Certain relevant critiques of ESD practices were also discussed. Traditional Buddhist ecological wisdom was offered in considering these sustainability issues, which are generated from a belief in humans' dual relationship with nature. In nature, nothing can be conquered; only our dualistic thinking can be overcome. Based on this thinking, the no-self might offer us a sustainable approach for living in nature and act as a therapy for our egocentrism towards the outside world. If people realise that there is no identity of the self, then every being in the natural world becomes an integral part of the self. Nature has its inner order for maintaining constancy in its operations. The actual sustainability is that no sustainability exists in mind. Sustainability is not a name based on anthropocentric view; it is simply natural progression. Concerning the aim of sustainability, a vital question is what we should seek to 'sustain'. When viewed broadly, ESD promotes the development of humans and non-humans. They can never be dichotomised; both are merged into a natural oneness, in a natural everlasting.

Disclosure statement

No potential conflict of interest was reported by the author.

Funding

This research was sponsored by the Ministry of Science and Technology, Taiwan [project number 104-2410-H-019-018].

References

Bonnett, M. (2006). Education for sustainability as a frame of mind. *Environmental Education Research, 12*, 265–276. doi:10.1080/13504620600942683

Bonnett, M. (2009a). Systemic wisdom, the 'selving' of nature, and knowledge transformation: Education for the 'greater whole'. *Studies in Philosophy and Education, 28*, 39–49.

Bonnett, M. (2009b). Schools as places of unselving: An educational pathology? In G. Dall'Alba (Ed.), *Exploring education through phenomenology. Diverse approaches* (pp. 28–40). Malden, MA: Wiley-Blackwell.

Bonnett, M. (2013b). Normalizing catastrophe: Sustainability and scientism. *Environmental Education Research, 19*, 187–197. doi:10.1080/13504622.2012.753414

Bonnett, M. (2013a). Sustainable development, environmental education, and the significance of being in place. *Curriculum Journal, 24*, 250–271. doi:10.1080/09585176.2013.792672

Clarke, P. (2012). *Education for sustainability: Becoming naturally smart.* Oxon: Routledge.

Danvers, J. (2009). Being–in-the-world: The ability to think about the self in interconnection and interdependence with surrounding world. In A. Stibbe (Ed.), *The handbook of sustainability literacy* (pp. 186–190). Cambridge: Green Books Ltd.

Filho, L. W., Manolas, E., & Pace, P. (2009). Education for sustainable development: Current discourses and practices and their relevance to technology education. *International Journal of Technology and Design Education, 19*, 149–165. doi:10.1007/s10798-008-9079-z

Hyland, T. (2015). On the contemporary applications of mindfulness: Some implications for education. *Journal of Philosophy of Education, 49*, 170–186.

King, S. B. (2009). *Socially engaged Buddhism.* Honolulu: University of Hawai'i Press.

Loy, D. R. (2003). *The great awakening: A Buddhist social theory.* Boston, MA: Wisdom Publications.

Murray, P. (2011). *The sustainable self: A personal approach to sustainability education.* London: Earthscan.

Nan, H. C. (2004). *Diamond sutra explained.* (H. En, Trans.). New Jersey, NJ: Primordia Media. (Original work published 1975).

Newton, L. H. (2003). *Ethics and sustainability: Sustainable development and the moral life.* Mahwah, NJ: Prentice Hall.

Nhat Hanh, T. (2008). *The world we have: A Buddhist approach to peace and ecology.* Berkeley: Unified Buddhist Church.

O'Donnell, A. (2015). Contemplative pedagogy and mindfulness: Developing creative attention in an age of distraction. *Journal of Philosophy of Education, 49*, 187–202.

Orr, D. W. (1992). *Ecological literacy: Education and the transition to a postmodern world.* New York, NY: State University of New York Press.

Shiva, V. (1992). Recovering the real meaning of sustainability. In D. E. Cooper & J. A. Palmer (Eds.), *The environment in question: Ethics in global issues* (pp. 187–193). London: Routledge.

Stables, A. (2013). The unsustainability imperative? Problems with 'sustainability' and 'sustainable development' as regulative ideals. *Environmental Education Research, 19*, 177–186. doi:10.1080/13504622.2012.729813

Sterling, S. (2009). Ecological intelligence. In A. Stibbe (Ed.), *The handbook of sustainability literacy* (pp. 78–83). Cambridge: Green Books Ltd.

Suzuki, D. T. (2006). The role of nature in Zen Buddhism. In W. Barrett (Ed.), *Zen Buddhism: Selected writings of D.T. Suzuki* (pp. 275–310). New York, NY: Three Leaves Press.
UNESCO. (2012). *From green economies to green societies: UNESCO's commitment to sustainable development.* Retrieved from http://unesdoc.unesco.org/images/0021/002133/213311e.pdf
World Commission on Environment and Development (1987). *Our common future.* Oxford: Oxford University Press.

Harmonizing ecological sustainability and higher education development: Wisdom from Chinese ancient education philosophy

Xiaoxia Chen

ABSTRACT

Ecological sustainability can be considered the primary goal of higher education development, as it provides an ontological way to think about what it means for higher education's long-term development. Given the widespread concern of ecological sustainability, it's urgent to interpret and deconstruct ecological sustainability in Chinese higher education from indigenous and original perspectives. By drawing on the wisdom from Chinese ancient education philosophy which provides unique enlightenment for ecological sustainability, this paper discusses the harmonization of ecological sustainability and higher education development. In the light of the connotation of contemporary ecological sustainability and the new development of Chinese higher education, the paper also constructs a dynamic model of ecologically sustainable development in Chinese higher education. The aim is to initiate more philosophical dialogues between ancient and modern education, and to provide a new way of conceptualizing Chinese ancient education philosophy in the postmodern times.

Introduction

Since the 1960s, the global ecological environment has been seriously damaged by the aggravation of ecological crisis, which has been related to the survival of all mankind (Carchidi, 2006). Just as Fotopoulos (2007) articulates, 'a major dimension of the present multidimensional crisis, is the ecological crisis, namely the crisis which concerns our interaction, as social individuals, with the environment' (p. 1). Ecological crisis affects people's world view of taking man as the foundation deeply, resulting in a great conversion in human beings' understanding of development (Hunnicutt, 2011). All these make it clear that environmental and population education is a matter of cardinal significance in solving ecological problems of modern society. Education, at all times, has never existed in isolation, and it can take place in formal or informal settings and any experience that has a formative effect on the way one thinks, feels, or acts (Dewey, 2008). It is, in a sense, the practical activity of human beings to transform themselves and the nature (Lai & Wang, 2015). Education in general should have the ambition to 'bring a range of searching questions about nature to the attention of learners, and to encourage them to develop their own on-going responses to those questions' (Michael, 2007, p. 710). Therefore, ecological education theory emerges as the times require, and ecological education movement develops vigorously.

In the 1990s, the ecological education movement almost touched every aspect of social life, and most countries in the world had shift their focus from purely concerning about the ecological environment to making joint efforts for sustainable development of society. Later, with the popularity of ecology, educators applied the theory of ecology to education, showing solicitude for the ecological development of education itself. The development of ecology of education promotes the transformation from traditional education development view to ecological view, which is the ecological trend of the international education development at present.

In the 1990s, the concept of sustainable development was put forward in Chinese higher education, with the focus of providing services and exploration for the sustainable development of society and higher education. Unfortunately, China's ecological sustainable development has always been biased towards the protection of natural environment and ecological balance, paying no more attention to ecological sustainability between human society and nature. In recent years, China has stepped into the stage of mass higher education in consequence of the increase of colleges and universities, and the expansion of enrollment. The rapid expansion of higher education inevitably brings about various problems and challenges, which are mainly represented in its inadaptability to economic and social development, and a large gap between Chinese higher education and excellent ones in the world. How to make a breakthrough in promoting the connotative development of Chinese higher education is an inevitable requirement of the sustainable development of higher education.

Under this background, a new interdisciplinary perspective is urgently needed to interpret ecological sustainability of Chinese higher education. Based on the theory of ecological sustainability and the wisdom of Chinese ancient education philosophy, this paper attempts to explore how to construct a dynamic model of ecologically sustainable development in Chinese higher education. The thrust of this paper is therefore to initiate more philosophical dialogues between modern and ancient education, to provide some likely manners of achieving ecologically sustainable development for higher education organization and to promote the value realization of higher education. Premised on the above-mentioned objectives, some fundamental questions are inviting answers, in order to have a clear-cut understanding of the necessity to harmonize ecological sustainability and higher education development. They are as follows:

1. What is the connotation of ecological sustainability that explain why there is the need to reconcile higher education to develop ecologically and sustainably?
2. What is the wisdom of Chinese ancient education philosophy that provides unique enlightenment for ecological sustainability?
3. What are likely manners of harmonizing ecological sustainability and higher education development?

The connotation of ecological sustainability

Sustainability under that name was inspired by ecologists, which has become a comprehensive, multi-dimensional concept, and been widely used in economics, sociology, development and other disciplines. In ecology, sustainability is in general terms the property of biological systems to remain diverse and productive indefinitely. Traditionally, it has different implications for people with different social responsibilities. The most popularly quoted definition of sustainability is that from the Brundtland-report *Our Common Future* (OCF) in 1987, which said sustainable development is development that meets the needs of the present without compromising the ability of future generations to meet their own needs. Unfortunately, the Brundtland definition of sustainability should not be considered as a timeless entity as OCF itself was a political compromise aiming at solving some problems at the time of publication (Magee *et al.*, 2013). At the 2005 World Summit on Social Development, sustainability was defined better, presenting it as an integration of social, economic, and environmental factors. Wandemberg (2015) defined sustainability as a socio-ecological process characterized by the pursuit of an ideal which is by definition unattainable in a given time and space. However, by persistently and dynamically approaching it, the process results in a sustainable system. A more complete definition of sustainability is thus environmental, economic, and social sustainability, which forms the goal of the three pillars of sustainability (Ralph, Harald, & Peter, 2012, p. 545).

On the basis of intensive study of sustainability, ecologists put forward the concept of ecological sustainability, which is open to many interpretations. But in general, it refers to 'an ecological adaptability of ecosystems to maintain their essential functions and processes, and retain their biodiversity in full measure over the long-term' (Northrop, 2013, p. 1784). As the basis of sustainable development of society, production and economy, ecological sustainability emphasizes the finiteness of the ecosystem, the global village, the resources and the environmental capacity. Ecological sustainability therefore is not merely about the integration of environmental, economic, and social problems, nor is it about widespread discussion and consultation. It is really about maintaining or sustaining something which will influence our generation and the future generations.

There are two core requirements for ecological sustainability which have been developed from the natural step system conditions. The first one is that 'the diversity of life and the basis of its productivity must be maintained', and the second one is that 'our society must be well organized' (Philip, 2000) so that it is easy to maintain the diversity of life and the basis of its productivity. Moving towards ecological sustainability is facing comprehensive challenges that entail some interconnected domains, such as politics, economics, culture and education, etc. Accordingly, ecological sustainability may take different forms from reorganizing living styles, encouraging ecological take-off in the economy and society to greening up culture. In recent years, the term has been applied to a broad range, from the initial ecology to society, agriculture, economy, education and other fields. Scholars at home and abroad have carried on the thorough study to it from different perspectives and levels. Educational discourse has also increasingly centred on the much-touted ecological sustainability to promote education to meet the demands and challenges of contemporary society.

Bearing all these in mind, it is very pertinent to ensure that higher education should be ecologically sustained. This therefore spurs the need to have some insight into wisdom of Chinese ancient education philosophy, with a view to exploring how to harmonize ecological sustainability and higher education development.

Wisdom from Chinese ancient education philosophy

'It has always been a challenge to define Chinese philosophy of education, especially in modern times where educational practices are influenced by the diverse and miscellaneous relevance of the global village' (Hung, 2018, p. 3). Many scholars still think Chinese philosophy of education, in contrast to the western educational philosophy, is strongly attentive to the issues of cultivation of the self, the social order and the harmony between human beings and nature (Guo, 2000; Hung, 2018; Ivanhoe, 2000; Tu, 1999). With the increasing studies of comparative philosophy, it is indeed a hopeful anticipation to revitalize ancient Chinese educational thought and provide unique enlightenment for the contemporary world.

The essence of Chinese ancient education philosophy is the harmony between humanity and nature (Tien-Ren He Yi天人合一) and the unity of knowing and doing (Zhi Xing He Yi 知行合一), which is also the core idea of Chinese traditional culture (Huang, 2008). Chinese ancient thought is taken as comprising environmentally friendly doctrines and values, which has great influence on today's world. However, the deteriorating ecological and environmental crisis in modern China, combined with the development of science and philosophy, really causes people to reflect on some important questions. Is the archaic idea of Chinese education philosophy workable in modern societies characterised by digital technologies, capitalist marketisation, and globalization? What is the value of ecological sustainability in Chinese higher education? How do ecological sustainability of higher education development resonate with the wisdom of Chinese ancient education philosophy? Can our understanding of ecological sustainability in higher education be refreshed by the vision expressed in Chinese ancient education philosophy? Furthermore, what is its implication for contemporary education worldwide? Such questions are educationally relevant because they not only represent important patterns of vocalizing our ideas of the human situation, but also provide an exciting opportunity to re-focus education under the new situation. These are major issues that educators must emphasize when they reinterpret and reconstruct Chinese higher education with respect to ecological sustainability. Just as Chinese philosopher Chen (2015) suggested, the key to the classics is to understand their meaning in the ancient social context as well as how they relate to contemporary social life.

As an important part of Chinese traditional philosophy, Chinese traditional philosophy of education originates from Confucian education philosophy, predominantly from Simeng School (Simeng Xue Pai 思孟學派) (Liang, 2002, p. 27). Due to its particularity, Chinese ancient education philosophy could broadly include 'philosophical discussion and reflection of education based on Chinese thoughts but with considerations of the influence of the West or with the interaction between Chinese and non-Chinese cultures' (Hung, 2018, p. 3). Through continuous creation and innovation, typically Chinese concept of educational philosophy has finally come into being, providing beneficial references for the reinterpretation of modern education. Without any doubt, in the matter of solving current ecological crisis, scientific and philosophical issues, Chinese traditional philosophy of education has unique value. It can provide an alternative lens to view and ponder the limitation of higher education development in modern society.

There have been widely differing versions about the basic characteristics of Chinese ancient education philosophy. From the overall framework, Zou (2005) induces several basic characteristics of Chinese ancient education philosophy, such as the harmony between humanity and nature, the unification of politics and religion, and the unity of knowing and doing, etc. Compared with western philosophy of education, Chinese ancient education philosophy 'lays stress on morality, harmony, accumulation, synthesis and entirety, but unfortunately neglects utility, competition, discovery, analysis and individuality' (Guo, 2000, p. 3). Through the integration of macro-examination and micro-examination, the basic characteristics of Chinese traditional philosophy of education can be observed from a new perspective, which will give it a fresh meaning of the time. In the sections that ensue, in addition to the discussion of its basic characteristics, the resonances between Chinese ancient education philosophy and ecologically sustainable development of modern higher education will be illustrated.

Comprehensive view

The first characteristics of Chinese ancient education philosophy is the comprehensive view, that is, the concept of macro-education. Education is regarded as a subsystem of social system in Chinese traditional education. Many educational problems are essentially social problems, and therefore 'must be investigated and solved in social system' (Zou, 2005, p. 138). The great sage in ancient China, Confucius, attaches great importance to education which is regarded as one of three indispensable elements of building up the nation (*Analects* 13.9 and 15.39). He holds that the only important thing is to develop education after people are well-off (*Analects* 13.9). In fact, Confucius goes so far as to 'provide education for all people without discrimination' (You Jiao Wu Lei有教無éj) (*Analects* 15.39). Furthermore, Confucius in particular thinks highly of the education of social morality and family ethics (*Analects* 1.2, 4.5 and 7.6). A highlighted point of his ideas is to emphasize the important role of education to govern the country and maintain social order. Citing Confucius, he argues that 'people should be guided by morality and etiquette, rather than law and corporal punishment' (*Analects* 2.3). It is very profound to regard personal moral cultivation and the improvement of social moral standards as the basis of governing the country and keeping social peace.

In the same way, *Xueji* (學記), the earliest treatise on education and teaching in ancient China, even in the world, generalizes the social function of education into two interrelated aspects: cultivating the talents needed by the country and shaping positive social morality (Liu, 1984). As *Xueji* (1) says 'education is the only way to influence people and develop good customs'. A more familiar expression of this idea is 'founding a country, teaching first (建å君民,教學爲先)' (*Xueji,* 2). This can be regarded as the classical generalization and summary of the social function of education in Chinese traditional education, which also provides profound reference to education today.

To recapitulate, the comprehensive view of Confucian education philosophy resonates with ecological sustainability' call to maintain the integrity and interdependence of the earth. For the modern higher education, its ecological sustainability is not the rapid expansion of college size and students number, but the comprehensive and harmonious development with the social ecological environment . Furthermore, this Confucian emphasis on education resonates with the cultural function of higher education to promote and develop humanistic spirit and ecological consciousness.

Dialectical view

The second characteristics is dialectical view, namely, the concept of the unity of opposites. Chinese ancient education emphasizes the importance of moral education, moreover, it also does not ignore the role of knowledge education. This has been seen very clearly when Confucius declares that 'A princely man is fond of virtues (Jun Zi Huai De君子æ·德)' (*Analects* 4.11). And he goes a step further to argue that 'those who love benevolence not learning will be fooled by others (好仁不好學,其蔽也愚)' (*Analects* 17.8). In addition, 'for Confucius, it is important to learn a knowledge core of the classical texts, such as the *Odes* or the *Shijing* (詩經), a collection of three hundred songs and poems sung at religious and court ceremonies in early China' (Tan, 2016, p. 3). This Confucian emphasis on morality and knowledge resonates with the call of Dong Zhongshu (a famous philosopher and Confucianist in the Western Han Dynasty) – the unity of benevolence and knowledge. He declares that benevolence without knowledge cannot help people distinguish between good and evil, knowledge without benevolence cannot promote great success (Yan, 2003). Furthermore, benevolence and knowledge are of dialectical unity which have their inherent consistency and ultimate goal. The unified view of morality and knowledge in Chinese ancient education interprets well the mutual dependence, mutual penetration, mutual influence and unity of opposites of intellectual education and moral education.

Similarly, there are dialectical relations, both contradictory and unified, between knowledge and ability. A highlighted point of *Xueji* (學記) is to emphasize the holistic relationship between teaching and learning in Chinese ancient tradition (Xu & McEwan, 2016, p. 10). It says: 'Teaching and learning are two halves of a whole that inform each other (Xiao Xue Ban æ學半)' (Liu, 1984, p. 122). A more familiar expression of this idea is 'teaching and learning complement each other (Jiao Xue Xiang Zhang教學相長)' (Xu & McEwan, 2016, p. 10). The idea that teaching benefits teachers as well as students implies not only the unity of opposites between teaching and learning, but also the equal and mutual promotion between teachers and students. This profound dialectics in Chinese traditional education is very rare, even in the monographs of modern education. Notwithstanding the venerable oriental features of Chinese traditional education philosophy, indeed it provides fresh perspectives in the notion that education is pursuing all-round development in the unity of opposites. More precisely, Chinese traditional education philosophy buttresses ecological sustainability in modern higher education in its emphasis on the interrelated and dynamic relationship between teaching and learning.

Intrinsic view

The third characteristics is the intrinsic view, which emphasizes humanity and the inner moral initiative. This is highlighted in the Confucian texts, where Confucius declares that 'A princely man is fond of virtues (Jun Zi Huai De君子æ·德)' (*Analects* 4.11), and hopes the social system could be followed self-consciously by enhancing the moral initiative (*Analects* 12.1). Additionally, Confucius encourages to emulate those better than oneself (Jian Xian Si Qiè¦賢思齊) (*Analects* 4.17) and to pay more attention to self-cultivation (*Analects* 4.2, 4.6 and 4.11). Zeng Shen, one famous disciple of Confucius, reflects on himself many times a day (*Analects* 1.4). Furthermore, Confucius' discussions about *junzi* (君子) (*Analects* 4.11, 12.4, 13.3 and 24.12, etc.) give prominence to this remarkable characteristic. As Guo (2000, p. 2) discusses, Chinese traditional education was neither pessimistic nor heteronomous. Rather, it was optimistic and self-disciplined, different from western traditional education: western traditional education advocates looking for standards from God, whereas Chinese traditional education emphasizes strengthening self-cultivation in daily life.

This Confucian emphasis on inner moral initiative, from self-benevolence (Wei RenYou Ji爲仁由己) (*Analects* 12.1), introspection (Zi Xing自省) (*Analects* 4.17) and self-discipline (Shen Du 慎ç") (*Book of Rites*) to self-realization (Zi Cheng 自成) (*The Doctrine of the Mean*) evokes a better understanding of Bragg's concepts of self-realization and the ecological self. As Bragg (1996, p. 100) states, this kind of self-realization and the ecological self is 'the manner to realize human inherent potentialities in educational practices'. The consistent view of the philosophy of the east and the west resonates with the fundamental principles of ecological education, which emphasizes the naturalness of human beings and people-oriented education. According to educational ecology view, the naturalness and individual differences of the educated should be fully esteemed to promote their initiative and ecological development (Wu & Zhu, 2000).

To summarize, it is clear therefore that the basic connotation of Chinese ancient education philosophy resonates with ecologically sustainable development thought that the earth is holistic and interdependent. Chinese ancient education philosophy is momentous to revive ancient Chinese educational thought and explore new meanings for the contemporary education. It sets an excellent example of 'how to make the classics relevant to the contemporary educational world, both in China and abroad' (Tan, 2016, p. 10). The essence of ancient thought provides theoretical foundation for the higher education development in terms of the sustainable and ecological environment. Consequently, it has become a hot topic to discuss sustainable development by using Chinese ancient education philosophy. It must be stressed, however, that in its resonance with ecological sustainability, Chinese ancient education philosophy is not omnipotent to solve environmental and development problems facing the entire human race. What we should do therefore is to combine the excellent culture in the philosophy of the east and the west, thereby jointly establish a harmonious view of human and nature under the new conditions.

Harmonizing ecological sustainability and higher education development

A complete ecosystem is assumed to 'be the one that will regulate itself because the biosphere is an active adaptive control system able to maintain the earth in homeostatic' (Ojedokun, 2014, p. 122). Unfortunately, the ecosystem has been altered and the conflict between environment and development is still relatively intense. People concerned about ecological environment therefore should mediate and perhaps reconcile the conflict.

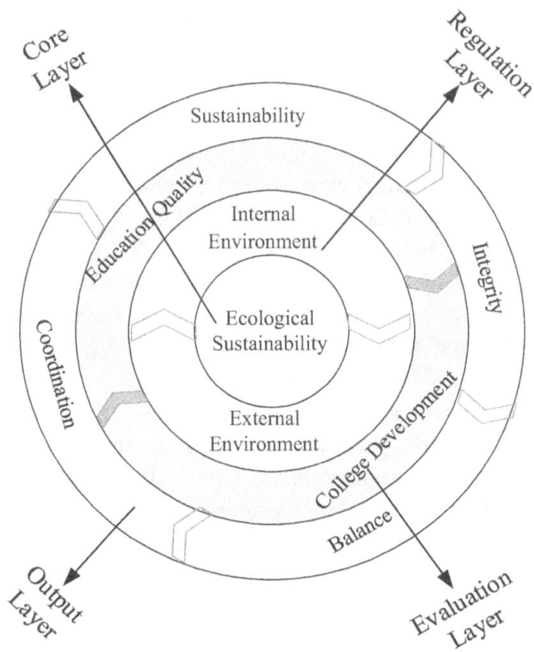

Figure 1. Ecologically sustainable development model of higher education.

Having shown how Chinese ancient education philosophy resonates with higher education' call to develop ecologically and sustain-ably, I turn now to the key problem, that is, the harmonization of ecological sustainability and higher education development. It is been accepted widely that higher education is essentially an ecological and sustainable education. Therefore, 'harmonizing ecological sustainability and higher education development' means higher education should develop both ecologically and sustain-ably in this paper. Based on a brief summary of ecological sustainability in higher education, a dynamic model has been constructed in order to explain the basic characteristics and evolution mechanism of ecological sustainability in higher education development.

Ecological sustainability in higher education

The ecological environment of higher education system is a multi-dimensional environment, consisting of natural environment, social environment and normative environment. Higher education system and its ecological environment constitute the ecological system of higher education, which is a systematical project. Ecological sustainability in higher education means bringing higher education into social ecosystem from the perspective of ecology and systematics. Generally speaking, its connotation includes three aspects: the people-oriented concept, the coordination between higher education system and external ecological environment, and the coordinated development within higher education ecosystem.

Ecological sustainability in higher education has concordant features with sustainable development of education: the balance of educational ecology, the sustainability of educational development, the integrity of educational function, the competitiveness of education system, etc. Among all these features, the balance of educational ecology is the most important one. Similarly, its ecological balance mainly depends on the exchange relationship between system and environment, and the balance of structure and function of higher education system. The sustainable development of education ecosystem is one of the important premises to keep the ecological balance of education. How to guarantee ecological sustainability in higher education is a systematic project, which needs supports in many ways.

He (2005) discusses that the higher education ecosystem is not a purely natural ecosystem, but an artificial ecosystem intervened and regulated by scientific means. The relative stability of its structure and function can be enhanced by rational organization and regulation of human beings. Furthermore, higher education system is a social ecological system which consists of human, education and environment. It is full of paradoxical movement between adaptation and development, balance and unbalance, symbiosis and competition. Therefore, the relative stability of the quality of higher education is an important indicator to measure the ecological balance of higher education system in a certain period. In order to strengthen quality management and ecological evaluation, and then to promote higher education development, systematic and scientific quality control and evaluation mechanism count for a great deal.

Dynamic model of ecologically sustainable development in Chinese higher education

Dynamic model is created to express the static and dynamic behavior of the system, which can provide different viewing angles for the system. It mainly describes the system characteristics, event environment, event sequence and control logic of the system. To reveal the logic relationship of ecological sustainability in Chinese higher education, it is necessary to fully consider its dynamic mechanism.

Integrating Sterling and Thomas's model (2006) and wisdom of Chinese ancient education philosophy, an ecologically sustainable development dynamic model of higher education was developed, in order to provide a tentative, theoretical frame of for Chinese higher education. As shown in Figure 1, the model is dynamic and cross-level which takes ecologically sustainable development as the core. It is intended as a dynamic and netlike system for explaining the integration and dynamicity of ecologically sustainable development model of higher education.

In this model, ecologically sustainable development is the core layer of the dynamic model, which is also the core goal of Chinese higher education. Higher education is essentially a sustainable and ecological education. Therefore, ecologically sustainable development of higher education is to integrate higher education into the social ecosystem from the perspective of ecology and systematics, which resonates with the comprehensive view of Chinese ancient education philosophy.

The regulation layer combines internal and external environment regulation to enhance the relative stability of structure and function of higher education's ecologically sustainable development. In general, the internal environment regulation includes physical environment, organizational environment, normative environment and educational content environment regulation. The external environment regulation is mainly the regulation of political environment, economic environment and cultural environment.

The essential function of evaluation layer is to ecologically evaluate higher education and effectively improve higher education quality. The diversification of higher education quality will inevitably lead to that of evaluation methods (He, 2005). Therefore, establishing a systematic and scientific quality evaluation mechanism is an effective way of higher education quality management. In general, the evaluation layer involves ecological evaluation of education quality and that of college development. By combining the views and methods of ecology and pedagogy, ecological evaluation of higher education is to evaluate higher education itself and its ecological environment, judge the dynamic process of educational ecology correctly and make prediction and decision-making scientifically.

The output layer that includes the sustainability of educational development, the balance of educational ecology, the coordination of educational development, and the integrity of educational function indicates the ultimate target and distinctive features of ecologically sustainable development of higher education. As a dynamic concept, the sustainable development of higher education system should change with that of ecological environment. Consequently, ecologically sustainable development, the core goal of higher education, is the dynamic balance of internal and external ecological environment of higher education. This kind of dynamic balance should be based on the elastic limit of self-regulation and self-adaptation of higher education. The coordination of educational development consists of two aspects: the coordinated development of the structure, scale, quality and efficiency of higher education, and the coordinated development of higher education and social economy. The integrity of educational function means that the effects of educational functions are interrelated and integrated. The individual and social functions of higher education have their integrity. Therefore, any deficiency of educational function will result in its loss in integrity.

Philosophically, the designed model which is expressed as netlike system with the interaction of four layers fully demonstrates the comprehensive view in philosophical dialectics. Ecologically sustainable development of higher education is not isolated from social ecosystem. On the contrary, it is the integration of higher education into the whole society development, which resonates with the comprehensive view of Chinese ancient education philosophy. Moreover, the designed model is the embodiment of the ontological and subject-object relationship in philosophy. According to the ontology, man belongs to nature and there is also subject-object relationship between man and nature. In these two kind of relationships, undoubtedly, the freedom and beingness of nature is fundamental . The freedom and beingness of nature ultimately determines the limits of their subject-object relationship. Ecologically sustainable development of higher education is the harmonious development on the premise of ecological balance, which coincides with the dialectical view of Chinese ancient education philosophy.

While still in its infancy, the designed dynamic model can be beneficial and instrumental to higher education development by providing a schematic for developing a culture of ecological sustainability. Of course, it is only a tentative theoretical framework which wants practice test. Aiming at the practical problems existing in higher education, He (2005) combines empirical method and statistical quantification to propose the concrete measures, in order to promote the ecologically sustainable development of Chinese higher education. These measures facilitate a coordinated and co-operative approach to ecologically sustainable development of higher education and encourages long-term benefits for higher education over short-term gains.

Conclusion

It is noticeable from the foregoing that higher education development is at a serious hot and cold war with ecological sustainability. Ecological sustainability challenges are closely interconnected, yet often separately studied and managed. Fortunately, Chinese ancient education philosophy has a positive significance to harmonize ecological sustainability and higher education development. There can be no doubt that the essence of these ancient thoughts provides a historical reference for the construction of modern humanistic spirit. This, in turn, necessitates a reinterpretation and perhaps a reconstruction of ecological sustainability in higher education. Thankfully, since the early 2000, the pursuit of ecologically sustainable development has been increasingly incorporated into the policies and programs of Chinese higher education as a significant policy objective.

Seeking source of originality from ancient Chinese philosophy of education, this paper attempted to discuss the harmonization of ecological sustainability and higher education development, then to construct ecologically sustainable development dynamic model of higher education under the new situation. It is hoped to make a rational analysis of higher education from the perspective of traditional philosophy of education, and to enlighten ecologically sustainable development of higher education with rational wisdom of ecology.

Disclosure statement

No potential conflict of interest was reported by the author.

Funding

This work was supported by MOE (Ministry of Education in China) Project of Humanities and Social Sciences under Grant (No.17YJCZH026); the Social Science Research Project of Shandong Higher Education Institutions under Grant (No. J17RA044).

ORCID

Xiaoxia Chen http://orcid.org/0000-0002-1644-9684

References

Bragg, E. A. (1996). Towards ecological self: Deep ecology meets constructionist self-theory. *Journal of Environmental Psychology, 16*, 93–108.
Carchidi, V. K. (2006). Review of the state and the global ecological crisis. *Electronic Green Journal, 1*, 13.
Chen, S. M. (2015). *Doing Chinese philosophy: Some methodological thoughts*. Beijing, China: SDX Joint Publishing Company.
Dewey, J. (2008). Experience and education. *Educational Forum, 50*, 241–252.
Fotopoulos, T. (2007). The ecological crisis as part of the present multi-dimensional crisis and inclusive democracy. *International Journal of Inclusive Democracy, 3*, 1–28.
Guo, Q. (2000). Chinese traditional education philosophy and global ethics. *Education Research, 11*, 3–7.
He, Z. B. (2005). *On the ecology of higher education*. Guilin, China: Guangxi Normal University press.
Huang, J. (2008). *A general theory of educational philosophy*. Taiyuan, China: Shanxi Education Press.
Hung, R. (2018). Kaleidoscopic view of Chinese philosophy of education. *Educational Philosophy & Theory, 12*, 1–5.
Hunnicutt, G. (2011). Ecology and socialism: Solutions to capitalist ecological crisis. *Sociological Inquiry, 81*, 272–275.
Ivanhoe, P. J. (2000). *Confucian moral self cultivation*. Indianapolis, IN: Hackett Publishing.
Lai, L., & Wang, R. (2015). Knowledge and knowers: Towards a realist sociology of education. *Educational Philosophy & Theory, 29*, 1–5.
Liang, T. (2002). A study on SiMeng School. *History of Chinese Philosophy, 3*, 27–34.
Liu, Z. (1984). *The interpretation of Xueji*. Jinan, China: Shandong Education Press.
Magee, L., Scerri, A., James, P., Thom, J. A., Padgham, L., Hickmott, S., … Cahill, F. (2013). Reframing social sustainability reporting: Towards an engaged approach. *Environment Development & Sustainability, 15*(1), 225–243.
Michael, B. (2007). Environmental education and the issue of nature. *Journal of Curriculum Studies, 39*, 707–721.
Northrop, R. B. (2013). Ecological sustainability. *Encyclopedia of Quality of Life and Well-Being Research*, 1, 1784–1784.
Ojedokun, O. E. (2014). Reconciling ecological sustainability and human development. Ideas for environmental and sustainable development education. *Asian Social Science, 10*, 119–128.
Philip, S. (2000). *Ecological sustainability*. Retrieved from http://www.green-innovations.asn.au/ecolsust.htm
Ralph, H., Harald, A. M., & Peter, F. (2012). Principal sustainability components: Empirical analysis of synergies between the three pillars of sustainability. *International Journal of Sustainable Development & World Ecology, 19*, 451–459.
Sterling, S., & Thomas, I. (2006). Education for sustainability: The role of capabilities in guiding university curricula. *International Journal of Innovation & Sustainable Development, 1*, 349–370.
Tan, L. (2016). Confucius: Philosopher of twenty-first century skills. *Educational Philosophy & Theory, 48*, 1–11.
Tu, W. M. (1999). *Humanity and self-cultivation: Essays in Confucian thought*. Boston, MA: Cheng & Tsui Company.

Wandemberg, J. C. (2015). *Sustainable by design: Economic development and natural resources use*. Retrieved from https://www.amazon.com/dp/1516901789/ref=cm_sw_su_dp

Wu, D. F. & Zhu, W. W. (2000). *Ecology of education*. Nanjing, China: Jiangsu Education Press.

Xu, D., & McEwan, H. (Eds.). (2016). *Chinese philosophy on teaching and learning: Xueji in the twenty-first century*. Albany, NY: State University of New York Press.

Yan, L. (2003). *The translation of Chun Qiu Fan Lu*. Heilongjiang, China: Heilongjiang People's Publishing House.

Zou, W. (2005). Educational nativization: Seeking wisdom from ancient Chinese philosophy: Concurrently on the education methods of zhuang-tse. *Journal of Shandong Normal University, 50*, 136–140.

Index

Note: *Italic* page number refer to figures and page numbers followed by 'n' refer to end notes.

www.ingramcontent.com/pod-product-compliance
Lightning Source LLC
LaVergne TN
LVHW080659011026
849160LV00014B/1479
9781032088433